Series Editor : Paul Seligson

Evaluating your Students

Andy Baxter

Richmond
PUBLISHING

Richmond Publishing
19 Berghem Mews
Blythe Road
London W14 0HN

© Andy Baxter 1997
Published by Richmond Pubishing ®
First published 1997

ISBN:978-84-294-5067-5
Depòsito legal: M-14678-2010
Printed in Spain by Palgraphic, S.A.

Design	Jonathan Barnard
Layout	Gecko Limited
Cover Design	Geoff Sida, Ship Design

Illustrations	Gecko Limited & John Plumb

Dedication
To my father – a great educator.

Contents

Richmond Handbooks for Teachers: An introduction

This series presents key issues in English Language Teaching today, to help you keep in touch with topics raised in recent educational reforms. The books all contain a mixture of analysis, development work, ideas and photocopiable resources for the classroom. The key note throughout is what is **practical**, **realistic** and **easy to implement**. Our aim is to provide a useful resource which will help you to develop your own teaching and to enjoy it more.

While each of the books has been written for the practising English Language Teacher in the primary or secondary environment, they are also suitable for teachers of languages other than English, as well as for teachers of young adults, trainee teachers and trainers.

All classroom activities are designed for lower-level classes (from beginners to lower intermediate) as these form the majority of classes in both primary and secondary. Most of them can, however, be easily adapted to higher levels.

The books all contain:

- *a section of photocopiable activities and templates.* These are either for immediate classroom use (some with a little adaptation to suit your classes) or for use throughout the year, e.g. assessment record sheets or project work planners.

- *regular development tasks.* These ask you to reflect on your teaching in the light of what you have just read, and some ask you to try new ideas in the class. They are all intended to make the ideas in the books more accessible to you as a classroom teacher.

- *an index of topics/activities.* As most teachers dip into or skim through resource books, there is an index at the back of each book to help you find the sections or ideas that you wish to read about.

- *a comprehensive glossary.* As one of the main principles of the books is ease of use, the authors have tried not to use jargon or difficult terminology. Where this has been unavoidable, the word/term is in SMALL CAPITALS and is explained in the glossary at the back. Likewise, we have avoided abbreviations in these books; the only one used which is not in current everyday English is L1, i.e. the students' mother tongue.

Although all of the ideas in these books are presented in English, you may need to explain or even try some of them, at least initially, in the students' L1. There is nothing wrong with this: L1 can be a useful, efficient resource, especially for explaining methodology. New ideas, which may challenge the traditional methods of teaching and learning, can be very threatening to both teachers and students. So, especially with lower-level classes, you can make them less threatening by translating them. This is not wasting time in the English class, as these ideas will help the students to learn/study more efficiently and learn more English in the long term.

The problem of evaluating

"Who is this book for?"

One of the jobs we are always asked to do as teachers is to *assess* our students. In other words, we are required to say how good – or bad – they are. So any teacher can benefit from a book on testing.

If you are interested in finding out something about testing and applying it to your classes, then this is the book for you. If you are interested in improving testing techniques you already use and initiating new ways of testing, then it is for you. However, if you want a totally theoretical exposition of testing, then this book **isn't** for you.

Evaluating your students is intended for the teacher of secondary-level students, and the practical ideas contained within it are appropriate for teenagers, but could easily be adapted for older students. Testing young children, however, is a different matter and beyond the scope of this book.

◆ SEE *AN INTRODUCTION TO TEACHING ENGLISH TO CHILDREN* IN THE SAME SERIES

"I don't know anything about testing and I don't understand the terms."

Evaluating your Students starts by looking at what we assess and how we assess it, and tries to agree some terminology: what is the difference between testing and teaching, evaluation and assessment, measuring and judging? (CHAPTERS 1–3)

"How do I know if a test is 'good'?"

The traditional way to assess has been through using tests. Language testing is an academic area with a vast literature, very many theories, lots of statistics and its own journals. There is not enough room here to cover testing in great detail, so we will look at the basics: what you need to make a test good (CHAPTER 4). And we will see that it is difficult for any teacher or school to write a 'good' test.

"Are there different types of testing and evaluation?"

Perhaps the biggest difference between our old ideas about testing and newer ones about evaluation is that we have moved, as teachers and professionals, away from memorisation and towards helping students to learn: the procedures they use and the attitudes they bring to the class. Evaluation is bigger than just testing. CHAPTER 5 looks at the different forms of testing and evaluation.

There are so many abilities and skills that students have to learn, even in a single subject like a foreign language. How do we put them all together? Which skills are important and which skills can we afford to ignore? One way of thinking about the problem is to use the staff room as a parallel. You could try this rather dangerous game: Imagine your staff room, and all the teachers in it. One (rather drastic!) way of starting a discussion about evaluation would be to arrange all the chairs in a semi-circle. You then say you want the teachers to seat themselves in order of ability, with the 'best' teacher sitting in the chair at one end, and the 'worst' teacher sitting in the chair at the other end.

There would, of course, be huge uproar! How **do** you assess who is best and who is worst? But at least all the problems involved with assessment would come up in the argument. For example, some teachers are excellent at their subject but hopeless at paper work. Some have brilliant ideas but can't control a class, and so on. Are brilliant ideas worth more than class control or subject-area excellence?

"This is all theoretical. How can I put ideas about testing into practice?"

In order to assess learners and learning, we need some data about the student.

- Can he/she use the components of language – grammar, vocabulary, and pronunciation? (CHAPTER 6)
- Can he/she use the language itself – in reading, writing, listening and speaking? (CHAPTERS 7 – 9)
- How does he/she learn most effectively and can that become part of testing? (CHAPTER 10)

"And should I test the students at the end of the year, or twice a year, or more often?"

If we are interested in the student's development, we need to assess the student over a period of time. CHAPTERS 11 AND 12 look at CONTINUOUS ASSESSMENT and FORMATIVE EVALUATION: how we can record the student's progress in both language learning and in the skill of learning itself.

At some point, often the end of a course, we have to put a label on the student: what are his/her strong or weak points? In the past, both teacher and student would step back and let a test decide. We both surrendered responsibility.

"If testing is an individual activity, how can I assess a class of 30?"

This is impossible if you take on the role of assessor alone. But there are 31 people who can help each student: the teacher, the student, and all the student's peers. It **is** possible to evaluate large classes, but only if we re-examine responsibilities. If we do everything for the students, why should they bother to do it for themselves? In the case of compositions, we may spend 30 minutes marking work that the student wrote in ten. And every mistake that we find is something the student didn't find, or didn't bother to find.

"How can I get students more involved in the assessment process?"

It is time that we, as teachers, called on the students to share the responsibility for their assessment: however hard we try, we can't learn it for them! CHAPTER 13 looks at how this can be done. Sharing responsibilities means that both we and the students have to change. Change is a very threatening thing. It means we have to learn new skills, and we all worry that we won't be as good as we used to be.

"How do I use this book?"

Testing as problem solving

The quote below is from Arthur Hughes, in *Testing for Language Teachers* (page 6). He sees the language test not as something we can write and say this is how it is done, but as a problem to be solved.

Language testers are sometimes asked to say what is the best test or the best testing technique. Such questions reveal a misunderstanding of what is involved in the practice of language testing. In fact there is no best test or best technique. The assumption that has to be made therefore is that each testing situation is unique and so sets a particular testing problem. It is the tester's job to provide the best solution to that problem.

The same is true of all evaluation: there is no 'right' answer. There is only a problem, and the answer to that problem will almost certainly be different in your school with your staff and your students than in a school down the road. This book will try to explain the concepts and give you some ideas. But, inevitably, you may view many of the ideas in this book as 'idealistic', describing a 'perfect scenario'. It is up to you to use what you can, adapt what you can and omit what you know you can't do in your situation. Like all problems that affect lots of people, any solution will be the result of talking, arguing and final agreement. This might take some time to do, but we owe this to the students. Our assessments may affect their lives for years to come.

PART A Assessment, testing, evaluation

CHAPTER 1

Why do we assess students' learning?

There are many groups who have an interest in assessing a student's abilities: teachers, heads of departments, parents, governments and, of course, the students themselves. However, we all share the same four main reasons for assessment:

... to compare students with each other
... to see if students meet a particular standard
... to help the student's learning
... to check if the teaching programme is doing its job.

TASK

Write a list of the types of tests (not just foreign languages) given in your school. Why are they given? Which group is each one primarily aimed at? Who are the results for?

students teachers heads of departments parents governments others

1 To compare students with each other

If your students want to enter a university to study a popular subject, the university has to select which students it takes. It decides on a comparative basis, e.g. it wants the top 20% of candidates. But there is a problem: consistency. A good year of candidates may be compared with a weak year: this year's top 20% may not be as good as last year's top 20%. However, it is still the top 20% that get through the exam. This approach has been called 'rationing the carrots': however well all the candidates perform, only the top 20% get through.

Although this system may appear unfair, it is still often used by governments and parents to judge the quality of a school.

2 To see if students meet a particular standard

Large organisations, like the state, or international examining boards, have certain standards of proficiency that students must meet. These standards do not necessarily reflect the teaching programme that the students have followed: different schools may use different books or SYLLABUSES. So these large organisations have to set their own standards or criteria, and see if the student can perform at this level.

Other smaller organisations, like individual schools, can also set a particular standard based on their own individually-agreed criteria.

More frequently, though, schools will base their assessment on their own teaching programme. They analyse what the students cover in class, and then assess whether the students have learned it, often by giving an ACHIEVEMENT TEST.

Testers differ over what an ACHIEVEMENT TEST should actually cover. It could test **either**:

... the overall objectives of the SYLLABUS (e.g. in English, the ability to express past time, or the ability to write in a variety of styles), **or**

... the individual items on the SYLLABUS (e.g. in English, the past simple, or writing advertisements).

Another reason for assessment is initial placement. We can analyse the students' abilities in order to see where they fit into the system. For example, if the school has restrictions on space in classes, they may be placed according to what percentage they get (e.g. the top 10% go into the top class). Alternatively, there may be certain criteria the students are expected to meet. If one class concentrates on writing while another specialises in grammar revision, the students' class will be determined by their success according to these criteria.

3 To help the student's learning

Whether we assess proficiency or achievement, we can analyse the student's abilities in a diagnostic way. Instead of using the assessment to grade the student, we use it to see where the student needs more help. For example, the student gets an excellent grade in writing an advertisement, but makes many errors in the grammar section, especially in the present simple third person -s. We may then decide to give him/her additional help and teaching in this area.

4 To check if the teaching programme is doing its job

But suppose all the students get excellent grades in writing advertisements, but all make many errors in the present simple third person -s. We may then decide to alter the whole teaching programme to give all the students additional help and teaching in this area.

On a larger scale, if teachers and inspectors identify a common problem across all schools', a government may decide to alter the whole of its education programme.

Summary

There are, as we shall see in this book, many ways of assessing students. But probably the most common method of assessment is a test.

- PROFICIENCY TESTS examine a general standard in ability, regardless of the teaching programme.
- ACHIEVEMENT TESTS examine whether students can do what they have been taught, either by testing specific SYLLABUS items or general objectives.
- PLACEMENT TESTS are a mixture of the above two, depending on what criteria we use to place the student.
- DIAGNOSTIC TESTS use PROFICIENCY or ACHIEVEMENT TESTS to analyse strengths and weaknesses in the student or the teaching programme itself.

Think of two different tests that you know well: a language test or other test that is used in your school, and one of another subject or ability (like driving).

Is the test based on the teaching programme or not?

Who sets the test's standards/criteria?

How are the results used? To compare students? To assess the teaching programme? For other reasons?

CHAPTER 2

What's the difference between testing, teaching and evaluation?

What is testing?

Every time we ask students to answer a question to which we already know the answer, we are giving them a kind of test. Much of what we do in class is, in fact, testing students' knowledge. Here are some examples.

He goes to the cinema. They ...?
Find a word in the text that means 'angry'.
On the tape, where does John tell Susan he wants to visit?
What is the main idea of paragraph three?
Dictation: write down the following ...
That's that part of the lesson finished. What do you think we're going to do next?

Testing and teaching

Turning performance into numbers

Testing has, traditionally, measured the results of student performance.

- We choose some representative samples of language.
- We measure whether a student can use these samples.
- We then try to quantify this by turning it into a mark or grade.
- We keep a record of these marks and use this to give an end assessment.

Over time, all testing theory (whether languages or shampoo development) has traditionally been based on a semi-scientific procedure, namely:

1 Measure the performance.

2 Do something to affect the performance.

3 Measure the performance again and compare the difference.

Applying this traditional testing procedure or model to language learners has meant that the language learner is treated as a kind of plant. We measure the plant, apply the new fertiliser, and then measure the plant again to see what effect the fertiliser has had. As language teachers, we apply a (PLACEMENT) test, teach, and then give an ACHIEVEMENT TEST to see how much better the students are.

In other words, testing is generally concerned with ENUMERATION, that is, turning performance into numbers.

	Plants	Language learners
Stage 1	measure plant	test the present simple
Stage 2	add fertiliser	teach the present simple
Stage 3	measure plant again compare the difference	test the present simple again compare the difference

Testing activities and teaching activities

Teaching and testing go hand-in-hand. We often ask questions to check that the students have understood what we have said. Equally, we sometimes ask a question to find out whether we need to teach a point. We instinctively know why we ask a question: whether it is to teach or to test something.

Compare the following two exercises.

Exercise 1

Fill the gap with an appropriate form of the verb.

a John _____ France every year since 1993.   (visit)

b John _____ France last year.   (visit)

Exercise 2

In groups, discuss the differences between the two sentences.

a John has visited France every year since 1993.

b John visited France last year.

Exercise 1 assumes that the students have some knowledge and asks them to prove it. It is clearly a testing activity. Note that if the students get the right answer, we don't know why they wrote that answer. It may be a guess, or it might just sound right.

Exercise 2 asks the students a question about the language. In other words, it is asking them to formulate a rule they can use in other situations – a generalisable theory. It is also trying to increase their awareness of how the language works. It is trying to help them learn: it is a teaching activity. On the other hand, some teachers would say that people don't need to know why it is right, they just need to get it right.

Let's compare two more exercises.

Exercise 3

Composition: A Summer's Day at the Beach (150 words)

Exercise 4

Read the following two compositions entitled 'A Summer's Day at the Beach'. Which do you prefer and why?

Underline all the words and ideas relating to summer. Underline all the words and ideas relating to the beach. Put a tick next to the parts you like in each essay. Put a cross next to the parts you don't like in each essay.

If all the paragraphs got accidentally jumbled up, could you put them back in the right order? What would help you do this? Discuss your ideas with another group.

Homework: write your own composition on the same theme (150 words).

Using the same ideas as we outlined above, Exercise 3 is clearly a test: it wants the student to show us what he/she can do. Exercise 4, on the other hand, clearly tries to make the student more aware of what he/she is trying to do: it tries to increase awareness before giving the task. It tries to help the student to learn.

Teaching or testing?

Sometimes, though, teachers can get confused about whether they are teaching or testing. We can think we are teaching when we are actually testing.

This is particularly true when we try to teach the four skills: reading, writing, speaking and listening. Here language teachers face a major problem. We don't really know enough; that is, there are no clear rules about good listening, reading and other skills. All we have are some rather generalised ideas such as skimming and scanning, and these are not detailed enough to help us work out an effective and progressive teaching programme.

In other words, when faced with a skill that is difficult to teach, such as good listening, we normally answer this problem in one of two ways. **Either** we give the students lots of opportunities to show what they know so we can see if they're improving. We ask them to read, write or listen to texts of increasing linguistic complexity and hope they keep the same general results or even improve; or we keep the same texts and increase the complexity of the questions.

This is a bit like a doctor saying *I don't know what caused your illness or why you're getting better, but your temperature is going down*. All we can do to teach the four skills is expose students to language and take their temperature via testing to see if they're getting better.

Or we substitute the skill that is difficult to teach with one that is easy to teach.

While the rules for skills are not very clear, we do have some very good rules for grammar and vocabulary, which makes them easier to teach (however, writing a grammar/vocabulary test can be complex, as we shall see later). So we sometimes believe we are teaching or testing a skill, when really we are practising or testing grammar or vocabulary. For example, many speaking tests are disguised grammar revision: they can become an oral test of grammar. They don't test real speaking skills such as interrupting without causing offence at all.

Why is this? Because the semi-scientific plant model of testing which we looked at earlier has some major problems. The next part covers these problems.

Problems with testing

Problem 1: Skills into numbers

On PAGE 9, we saw that testing is based on an idea from science: measure, make changes, measure again and compare.

One problem with the scientific model is that not everything can necessarily be measured in this way. There are some things we can easily test in this way, e.g. the present simple third person -*s*.

But other skills are more difficult to measure. How, for example, can we quantify a student's ability to make useful contributions to the class?

- First, we would have to define 'useful' and 'contribution' in a way that we could measure them.
- We could define 'useful' as 'successfully explaining something to another student'.
- We could define 'contribution' as 'answering a question put to the whole class by the teacher'.
- We could now count how many times a student successfully answered a teacher's question and the majority of the rest of the class understood.

The problem with this is that we are now measuring how many times a student 'successfully answered a teacher's question and the majority of the rest of the class understood'. This is not necessarily the same thing as making a useful contribution to the class.

So there are two dangers when assessing skills that are difficult to measure.

- We may take something we all understand and re-define it to make it measurable; but, in doing this, we may change the very thing we are trying to measure.
- If something is too difficult to measure, we leave it out of the test – even if the skill is very important.

In the end, we arrive at a position where we are only measuring the easily-measurable, rather than assessing the performance we are trying to improve.

Listen to your colleagues having (L1) conversations in the staff room.

What percentage of their natural spoken language consists of full sentences?

What percentage consists of sentence fragments linked by intonational devices and *ums* and *ers*?

How often do you teach students to speak in fragmented sentences?

Other problems with testing

Problem 2: Results versus processes, what versus why

Another problem with this semi-scientific system of QUANTITATIVE MEASUREMENT is that it does not record QUALITATIVE DATA. Measuring will tell us if the plant has grown, but not why (or why not). It gives us information about the results, but doesn't tell us anything about the process.

In the example essay (SEE PAGE 10), we would get a much better idea of the student's abilities from Exercise 4, because we could see some of the processes behind the work, e.g. we could look at where the student put the ticks and crosses in the essays, and then see if and how these were reflected in his/her own essay.

Problem 3: Standardisation and odd results

A third problem with the scientific model is that the fertiliser given to the plant must always be the same, or the results cannot be compared. We must remove the variables in order to assess the success of the programme. It is difficult to see how this can work in teaching. In schools, all the teaching would have to be the same, or we couldn't really compare the progress of individual students. This model of testing therefore leads to rather authoritarian teacher-proof methodologies.

The scientific model is also more interested in general trends, and strange individual results are often ignored. For example, imagine that in a listening test all your students get 90%, but your best student only gets 10%. For us as teachers, it is that one odd result that we would want to investigate.

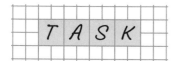

Choose a coursebook – perhaps the one used in your school – and select at random: three listening exercises   three reading exercises   three speaking exercises. What is the purpose of each exercise? Is it:

... testing grammar or vocabulary? (e.g. *Mr Brown _____ the cinema*; etc.)

... testing the student's understanding? (e.g. via multiple-choice questions about information in the text; information gaps; etc.)

... teaching the student to read/listen/speak better? (e.g. Does it include advice about how to improve reading or listening, practising interrupting, etc.)

... teaching the student to study? (e.g. Does it teach classroom language? Does it help the student to find answers to their own questions?, etc.)

Testing and evaluation

The relationship between testing and evaluation is similar to the relationship between the CURRICULUM and the SYLLABUS.

The SYLLABUS is a set of items for the teacher to cover in a term. But the SYLLABUS is part of a bigger methodological scheme – the CURRICULUM. A language teaching programme is not only **what** you cover (the SYLLABUS), but also **how** you cover it (the classroom procedures), and also **why** you cover it (the educational approach or rationale behind your SYLLABUS and classroom procedures).

Evaluation

In this book, we will see evaluation as wider than testing. Evaluation sees testing as a useful tool, but also thinks there are other important criteria for assessing someone's performance. We want to assess students' ability to use the present simple, but we also want other information about their (language) learning, e.g.

- Can they use a dictionary?
- Do they actually use the target language in class (e.g. for chatting)?
- Are their notes well organised?
- Do they contribute to groupwork?
- Are they well behaved?

If we compare this to the SYLLABUS–CURRICULUM diagram, we can see a (simplified) similarity:

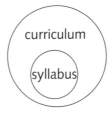 

Problems with testing: Can evaluation solve them?

Problem 1: Skills into numbers

Evaluation is not limited to numbers or just giving students marks. Instead of trying to count or measure a student's ability to make useful contributions to the class, we can simply judge whether he/she makes a contribution or not. In other words, you can be subjective as well as objective.

But when we make judgements, we must realise that other people, including teachers and students, may not agree with what we think. Evaluation means that sometimes we will have to justify, negotiate and possibly modify our opinions. We may need more than one judge – we may even need a jury.

Problem 2: Results versus processes, what versus why

In addition to ENUMERATION, evaluation looks for ILLUMINATION: *How did you learn that? Why did you write that?* We are doing something **with** the student, rather than doing something **to** the student. If we had to assess Miguel's performance over the year, would we rather have his essay from Exercise 3 (SEE PAGE 10), or his essay from Exercise 4 with his notes stapled to the back of it? Exercise 3 tells us *what*, but Exercise 4 tells us *what, how,* and *why.*

In addition, by asking these questions, we will learn a lot of extra information:

… what the student thinks he/she is learning

… what the student thinks is easy/difficult

… what the student enjoys/hates doing in class

... where the teaching programme and the student don't meet

... where the teaching programme needs to be re-designed.

In other words, we can use the assessment procedure to develop and improve not only the student, but also the teaching programme, and even the school. By evaluating procedures and attitudes, we gain more information – and more useful information – than by simply looking at test results.

Problem 3: Standardisation and odd results

Evaluation does not want to remove the variables in the assessment process. Evaluation is interested in odd results as it is exactly this kind of result that may illuminate something about the learning process. Equally, it does not want teacher-proof materials and methodologies. Instead, evaluation tries to include as many people as possible, because all information is seen as possibly useful for improving the design of a teaching programme.

Who evaluates?

As we will see in CHAPTER 4, writing a good test is an extremely complex task, and requires not only a lot of time and resources, but also some expertise in statistical analysis. For this reason, it tends to be large organisations such as governments and universities that write big tests, mainly because they need to keep the same NORM-REFERENCED standards year after year. ◆ SEE PAGE 31

With evaluation, however, we are trying to help the student to learn. Evaluation is not just an assessment, but an aid to learning. This means that the more people who are involved in the process, the better the process is.

Summary

As we have seen in this chapter, to teach students skills which are difficult to teach, we **either** ask them lots of questions (i.e. effectively micro-tests) to see if they're improving **or** we substitute the skill that is difficult to teach with one that is easy to teach.

To assess students in a skill which is difficult to measure, we **either** re-define it to make it measurable; but possibly change what we are measuring **or** we leave it out of the test and measure only the easily-measurable.

Testing also looks at the general, rather than the individual. Individuals, whether they are teachers or students, are variables that have to be removed from the assessment process. Individuals are turned into QUANTITATIVE data like results; and QUALITATIVE DATA, like processes or attitudes, are statistically removed.

Who can evaluate language learners?

The head of your school has decided to develop a new assessment system for the end of the next school year. He/She has asked you to provide a list of all the people who might have useful information about a student's language learning ability. Make an appropriate list, then consider the following questions.

What information could each group provide?

Given the system as it exists now, who would actually be consulted?

What information would you get using the present system?

What information would be missing, given the present situation?

Which parts of the missing information are the most important to include?

Can you think of any ways of incorporating these important areas into the present system without needing to re-design the whole assessment procedure?

CHAPTER 3

What do we assess?

Before we can assess a student's performance, we need to decide what we are going to assess.

At first sight, this looks like an easy question. As foreign language teachers we evaluate the student's ability in a foreign language. Earlier we gave the examples below as test questions (i.e. the teacher already knows the answers).

What do you think each of the following questions is actually **testing**? Think of your answers before you look at the key below.

1 He goes to the cinema. They ...?

2 Find a word in the text that means 'angry'.

3 On the tape, where does John tell Susan he wants to visit?

4 What is the main idea of paragraph three?

5 Dictation: write down the following ...

6 That's that part of the lesson finished. What do you think we're going to do next?

Key

1 This is testing grammar (using the present simple third person plural).

2 This is testing vocabulary (recognising that *furious* is a synonym of *angry*).

3 This is testing the student's ability to listen for detail.

4 This is testing either listening for general meaning or inferring from a text.

5 This is testing general ability (writing, reading, listening, pronunciation, spelling, etc.).

6 This is testing their ability to infer lesson phasing from their previous learning experience.

So we already test the students on a wide range of skills and abilities.

Message and medium

However, questions can have more than one answer. For example:

Teacher: *Miguel, where does the President of the United States live?*

Miguel (1): *He lives in London.*

Miguel (2): *He live in the White House.*

Miguel gives the teacher a problem here. His first answer is grammatically correct but factually wrong. His second answer is grammatically wrong but factually correct. Which answer is better?

The answer to this question is *It depends why you asked the question*. Language teaching is concerned with both message and medium. If we are testing the third person -*s*, Answer 1 must be correct. On the other hand, we are also trying to teach students to communicate in a different language. The grammatical mistake that Miguel makes in Answer 2 does not stop communication of the idea. Language teachers have to balance two different 'correctnesses': the right idea, i.e. the message and the right form of expression of that idea, i.e. the medium.

Which language abilities do we test?

Language components versus language use

Another common distinction is whether we assess the individual items that we put together to make a sentence, i.e. the components of a language (grammar, vocabulary, pronunciation); or whether we assess how the student puts these components together when they actually use the language (i.e. the four skills of speaking, listening, reading and writing).

Other skills of using language

We need to use language that is socially appropriate (e.g. formal versus informal vocabulary, etc.). We need DISCOURSE SKILLS: making what we say fit what has been said before (e.g. *I saw John. He said he was going to the cinema*, not *I saw John. John said John was going ...*). We need STRATEGIC SKILLS, too, such as how to take turns in speaking, get information from a text, listen for gist, etc.

Language learning skills

- the ability to use a dictionary
- the ability to work out meanings of unknown words
- learning metalanguage such as asking the teacher *What's the past tense of that verb?* etc.

General learning skills

- contributing to, and working in, groups in class
- the ability to know what you know and what you still need to learn
- strategies for finding information you don't know
- following the instructions in tests, etc.

Other behavioural or social skills

Many teachers would say that one of the primary skills for any learner is the ability, for at least part of the lesson, to stay sitting in his/her chair working rather than wandering around and disrupting the class.

Which of these abilities should we include in our assessment?
How much should each skill be worth?
And, if they are included, how should we record our assessment?

This takes us on to how easy or difficult these scores are to mark or record.

Other criteria for inclusion: Easy/difficult to mark or record

As we have already seen, there is also a problem about how to mark or record answers.

Assessments that give results as numbers (gap-fills, multiple-choice, etc.) are very easy to record. We can simply write the results (or RAW SCORES) on a piece of paper, or we can convert this number into a percentage, a mark out of twenty or an A–E grade.

Similarly, there are ways, as we shall see later (in CHAPTER 9), of marking writing, although these are much more complex as we are not counting correct results, but judging the quality of a piece of writing. We shall also see that the same systems can be used for other abilities, like speaking and behaviour.

However, when we want to assess, e.g. the student's contributions to the class, we have a bigger problem. This will almost certainly mean we will have to write notes. Notes are more difficult to record: different teachers will write different amounts about different things. If we want this information to be kept, we will have to have files for each student.

Summary

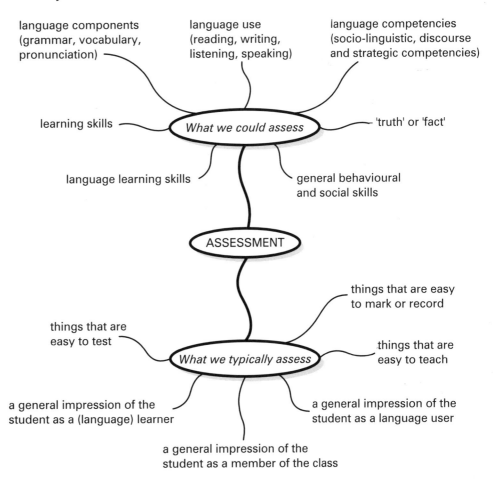

Think about your current system of evaluating a student at the end of the year.

Which of the skills mentioned above are included in your current assessment system? Which of the skills are not included? Can you think why they are not included?

Is one type of skill more valuable than another? For example, it gets higher marks, or determines the student's assessment?

How are these marks recorded?

Which skills are formally assessed (i.e. you record the information on the student's records)?

Which skills do think about when assessing the student, but are not recorded officially?

Does your present system work? Do the good students get through and the bad ones fail?

So how does your system define a good learner? Finish the sentence below:

In our school, a good learner is someone who can ...

CHAPTER 4

Testing: What makes a 'good' test good?

As we said in the Introduction, the easiest and most common form of assessment is to give the students a test. However, while writing a quick little test may appear easy, it is very difficult to write a good test. How much time and effort you invest in a test will depend on how important the result is to the student. If you want to know whether a student knows seven vocabulary items referring to *transport*, this is a simple test to write. The result isn't very important. For example:

> Write five more words in the same category:
>
> car, bus, _____, _____, _____, _____, _____

But if you are going to use the test to decide whether someone will repeat a school year, or will be able to go to university or not, the test obviously needs to be much better. These kinds of exam are normally written by international exam boards or by the state, simply because they are so complicated to make and score.

"So what is a good test?"　　A good test has the following qualities:

… it is valid

… it is reliable

… it is practical

… it has no negative effects on the teaching programme (negative BACKWASH).

Validity

There are three main types of validity:

CONTENT VALIDITY

CONSTRUCT VALIDITY

FACE VALIDITY

Before reading the sections below, look at the three types of validity above and have a guess what each type of validity means.

"What is content validity?"　　CONTENT VALIDITY means *Does a test test what it is **supposed to** test?*

For example, if we want to test whether a class of beginners can produce examples of the present simple for describing routines, we must make sure that:

… the questions are on the present simple for routines (and not, for example, present simple for future)

… we test the verbs that beginners are likely to know

… we ask the students to produce the answer, and not just recognise the answer by, say, using multiple-choice.

In other words, the questions we ask must be a representative sample of a beginner's whole ability to produce the present simple for routines.

It is easier to make the content of a test valid when we are trying to test small items like these. But CONTENT VALIDITY is more difficult to assure when we are testing a student's global abilities, as in a PROFICIENCY TEST. ◆ SEE PAGE 8

Let us look at a typical (lower) intermediate exam of general English. What structures do exams at this level typically test – and therefore assume are representative of a level of knowledge of English in general?

… modal verbs *can, must, don't have to*
… present perfect with *for*
… future *will* vs *going to*
… *-ed* vs *-ing* adjectives
… *-ing* form after verbs of liking and enjoyment
… *too* + adjective/*not* + adjective + *enough*
… simple passives, etc.

Yet it could test a number of other things, e.g.
… topic/comment sentences, e.g. *That car – it was awful.*
… colloquial English, e.g. *He gets on my nerves.*
… compound nouns, e.g. *table leg* vs *the back of the book*
… speed of delivery, e.g. average number of words per minute
… average sentence length
… turn-taking in conversation skills.

In other words, a test, especially a test of general English, cannot test everything. So we must choose a selection of things to test that we think are representative of a student's ability in knowing/using a (particular part of) language.

Note: Some skills are more difficult to test than others. Testing the passive is easier than, say, testing turn-taking in conversation. Similarly, some question-types are easier to write than others, e.g. you can listen to English for days without hearing anyone use reported speech, but it appears in lots of tests; not in order to test reported speech, but simply because it is useful for testing the student's ability to manipulate the tense system and (in questions) word order. They are very easy questions to write.

"What is construct validity?"

CONSTRUCT VALIDITY means *Does the test test what it's supposed to test and **nothing else**?*

Normally we try to test one of the following:
… grammar (i.e. structure, vocabulary and pronunciation)
… skills (i.e. reading, writing, listening and speaking).

But it is sometimes very difficult to test one of these without also testing others.

T A S K

Look at the following test question, then compare your answer with the notes on page 20.

Fill the gap with an appropriate verb in the correct form.

1) Mr Smith normally _____ a red Mercedes.

What must the student know in order to answer this question correctly? What exactly are we testing?

The student must:

… be able to read and understand the instructions. We are assuming that he/she understands the vocabulary (*appropriate*, *verb*, *form*).

… have some reading skills (e.g. he/she may speak English, but be illiterate).

… know the required vocabulary – and guess what the teacher wants. We may be trying to test if the student knows the verb *drive*, but he/she could use the verb *have* or *have got*.

… know the tense system. We want the 3rd person *-s*.

… also know what a 'Mercedes' is – we are using assumed cultural knowledge which the student may not have. Suppose in their country 'Mercedes' is a make of bike. Would we accept *rides*?

… also know some teacher-shorthand. We assume that if we write *normally*, the student will know that we want a present simple. But the student could write any of the following correct answers: *drove, used to drive, will drive, has driven, should have driven*, etc. (Although the word order should help them to choose.)

So if the student answers:

1 Mr Smith normally   *puts*   a red Mercedes.

How correct is this? How many marks do we give him/her?

1 mark for form? (the third person *-s* form is right)
1 mark for filling the gap? (he/she understood the instruction)
0 marks for appropriacy? (the verb is wrong)

"What is face validity?"

FACE VALIDITY means *Does the test **appear** to test what it is trying to test?*

For example, imagine that we do lots of research and we find that, amazingly, the size of a student's feet is directly related to language learning aptitude. We find that shoe-size is a better predictor of level than our own PLACEMENT TEST.

If this were true, it would make sense for us to throw away our PLACEMENT TEST and instead simply ask students *What's your shoe size?* Students, and parents, would immediately complain because there is no apparent link between shoe size and language ability.

In other words, there is a kind of psychological factor involved in testing. The test must appear to have something to do with the skill you are trying to test.

How to make tests valid: Content validity

Before you write a test, write down what you want to test.

- Do you want the students to recognise or produce the answer?

- Remember that one form (e.g. structure or vocabulary item) may have a number of different meanings.

- Remember that each structure or vocabulary item may have a number of different forms (singular, plural; questions, negatives, etc.; 1st, 2nd persons, etc.).

If you are testing a SYLLABUS, see what percentage of the SYLLABUS is given to each skill, form and meaning. If you are writing a general test, decide for yourself which skills, etc. are most important. You may find it useful to fill a chart like the one below and on PHOTOCOPIABLE PAGE 1.

Follow this procedure.

- Make a list of the teaching items on the SYLLABUS. An item might be the present simple, inviting or a vocabulary area.

- Then look at the amount of time the SYLLABUS or coursebook suggests spending on each item. Divide this by the total number of course hours or coursebook units, multiply by 100 and this will tell you what percentage of the course each item represents. (This method is, of course, relevant only if you are devising a test/tests for the **whole** SYLLABUS.)

- Then look at what forms of each item you have covered, e.g.

  Item: present simple
  1st/2nd/3rd person? singular/plural? questions/statements/negatives/ short answers?

  Item: vocabulary for food
  Singular/plurals? spelling? associated structures like un/countables?, etc.

  Item: inviting
  Which exponents? Which answers? (e.g. *Yes, I'd love to.*)

  Item: skim-reading
  What length of text? What speed? What text type?

- Then decide if the SYLLABUS expects the students simply to be able to recognise these items correctly used, or to be able to produce them.

You can fill out a kind of grid, e.g.

Syllabus item	What exactly are we teaching?	Percentage of syllabus	Recognise ✓/x	Produce ✓/x	Number of items in test
Grammar: *present simple*	*all persons, statements, questions, negatives and short answers*	15	✓	✓	*8/50*
Vocabulary: *food*	*countable/uncountable singular/plural*	5	✓	✓	*2/50*
Communication/function: *invitations*	*inviting accepting/refusing*	5	✓	✓	*3/50*

TIP

When you have completed the chart, you should try and make the number of questions and marks on each item match the percentages. Imagine, for example, that your complete beginner SYLLABUS recommends that you spend 15% of the time covering the present simple, and tells you that the students should be able to recognise the correct forms. You then look at the test and find that 50% of the questions relate to the present simple, and it includes gap-fills with no suggested answers. There is a clear mismatch between SYLLABUS and test.

How to make tests valid: Construct validity

Instructions

The easiest way in a monolingual classroom of removing any complications with instructions is to write them in the students' own language. On the other hand, test instructions are classroom-authentic items of the target language, and the ability to understand them becomes important if the students are to take international exams. A useful half-way point is to put both L1 and target-language instructions side-by-side, and to move gradually towards the target language ones over a number of years.

Remember to tell the students how many marks, or what percentage of their total score, each item/section is worth. This gives the student the responsibility of allocating an appropriate amount of time and effort!

Testing two things at the same time

Look at each question and check what you are trying to test. We can limit the student to make sure we are testing only the part we want to test, e.g.

> 1 Normally, Mr Smith _____ a red Mercedes.
> 2 Normally, Mr Smith _____ a red Mercedes. (drive)

In the last example, we must decide if we are testing *drive* or *-s*. If we give them *drive*, we are testing *-s*; if we don't, perhaps we should give a half-mark for *drive*, as the student has chosen the right vocabulary item.

Remember that *drove* is also correct. If more than one teacher is marking the exam, you will need an answer key and marking guide with all the possible answers. ◆ SEE SCORER RELIABILITY PAGE 26

How to make tests valid: In general

If possible, when you have written your test, check it with other people – native speakers, other teachers, and other students. Ideally, you should trial it with another class at the same level, and see if it gives results which are similar to other test results and the teacher's gut reaction. If you can't trial all of it, give the other class half of it, e.g. every other question.

Finally, check that your test looks like it is testing what you intend it to test. ◆ SEE FACE VALIDITY PAGE 20

For all these reasons, choosing some form of DIRECT TESTING (SEE PAGE 30) will normally automatically give you a more valid test (if the instructions are easily understood).

Reliability

There are two main forms of reliability:

TEST RELIABILITY

SCORER RELIABILITY

"What is test reliability?"

TEST RELIABILITY means *If it was possible to give the same person the same test at the same time, would the result be the same?*

Imagine you want to see how well people can play darts. You ask them to hit the bulls-eye. How many darts would they need to throw to convince you of their level of dart playing? Three? Five? Ten? For this example, we will choose five.

Now suppose you want to test if a student 'knows' the present simple. How many questions would you ask? We chose five for darts, so, if we want to test the third person *he*, we would need five questions or test items like:

> He _____ to the cinema every day.   (go)
> On Tuesdays, he _____ to go to the cinema.   (like)

Note: Because of CONTENT VALIDITY, we have to give them the base verb or we are also testing vocabulary.

But we can't assume that the student knows *she* as well as *he*. So we would need five *she* test items as well. And what about plurals? And names, as well as pronouns? And also things, possibly both concrete and abstract. In fact, we would need five test items for each of the following:

| *I* | *you* | *he* | *she* | *it* | *John* | *building* |
| *we* | *you* | *they* | *John and Mary* | *ideas* | | |

In addition, there are at least four forms of the present simple: statements, questions, negatives and negative questions. To make it simple, we will exclude question tags, *yes/no* answers, etc.

This means that, to test whether the student knows the present simple, we would theoretically need to ask the following:

12 subjects	x 4 forms	x 5 examples of each
I/you/he/she/it/we/you/they John/building John & Mary/ideas	affirmative/ negative/question/ negative question	

This gives us a test with 12 x 4 x 5 or 240 questions.

Remember that here we are only testing structure. The present simple can have many different meanings, apart from routine actions, including:

… universal truths (*The sun rises in the East.*)
… commentary or present historic (*Jones shoots and he scores! 2 – 1!*)
… futures (*Your train leaves at six a.m. tomorrow.*).

Imagine we wanted to test routine actions and these three other different meanings at the same time, we would need 240 x 4 questions – 960 in total!

However, we have to realise that this is totally impractical. So we have to compromise and select some of the possible questions we could ask. Out of the 240 possible questions we might ask 10 or 20. The problem is which 10 or 20 do we ask? We must hope that the sample we choose is representative.

Let us imagine two students: A and B. A only knows 20 answers out of the 240. B knows 220 answers out of the 240. It is therefore possible that lucky A might score 20/20 because we only ask the 20 questions he/she knows, but unlucky B might score 0/20 because we ask him/her only the 20 questions he/she doesn't know.

So here we are asking *How representative is our selection of questions out of all the questions possible?* Given our resources, there will always need to be a compromise between making our test long enough to be reliable but also short enough to be practical.

On the other hand, we must also make tests long enough to give enough samples to measure. For example, we can't test paragraphing skills unless the piece of writing is long enough to require paragraphs; and we can't test talking skills unless there is time to talk, interrupt, request information, and so on.

Sometimes we also need to make tasks sufficiently complex. You can't test a student's abilities to compare two possible choices and make an informed decision in a two-minute conversation about their summer holidays.

Of course, there has been a lot of research on TEST RELIABILITY and how to measure it, but it is all extremely complex and time-consuming. It is unrealistic to expect schools to have the time and resources to make a test totally reliable.

Instead, it may be best to accept that almost every test we design will have limited reliability. It will simply be a guide to the teacher when it comes to giving a final assessment of any student's abilities. And, if we are honest, if we think a student has under-performed in our reliable test, we are often still tempted to find a few marks and help them pass anyway!

How to make tests more reliable

Get enough examples

- See number of questions and complexity above.
- Give the students fresh starts. If they don't like the essay topic or question type, or if they feel they are making a mess of this question, they may not perform as well as they can. You need to let them start again on a fresh task. Compare Test A and Test B below.

Test A

> Write a letter to an aunt who is borrowing your family's house for a holiday. Tell her how your holiday is going and describe what there is to do in the area if she gets bored. As you are the only person in your family who knows how the video works, your parents have asked you to explain to her how to change channels and how to record a programme on a different channel from the one she is watching. (250 words)

Test B

> **a** Some relatives are staying in your house while you are on holiday. You are the only person in your family who knows how the video works. Your parents have asked you to write a short note telling them how to change channels and how to record a programme on a different channel from the one they are watching. Write a short note explaining how to do it. (75 words)
>
> **b** Write a short postcard to an aunt to tell her how your holiday is going. (75 words)
>
> **c** During the school holidays, you and your parents have moved to a new house in a different part of your city. You are writing to a friend who is away with his/her parents on their summer holidays. Write one paragraph from the letter describing what the new part of the city is like, and telling him/her what there is to do there. (75 words)

As you can see, the tasks are very similar; but Test B gives the student three fresh attempts at the same task, and also allows you to test a wider range of social styles, audiences, and text types.

Testing techniques

Make them:

- varied – don't use only one technique to measure. For example, don't use just gap-fills, but also other techniques such as multiple choice. However, don't give the answer to question 10 in question 24, e.g.

> Write the appropriate question word.
> **10** _____ does he go on Friday nights?
>
> Fill the gap with the appropriate form of the verb.
> **24** Where _____ he _____ on Tuesday mornings? (go)

- familiar – the students may not perform well if they have to learn new question-types in the middle of the test. Students should have met the question-type before. For example, if you normally only do true/false listening comprehension tasks, the following would confuse a student.

> Listen to the tape and decide if the information is true (**T**), false (**F**) or not given (**NG**).

Instructions

Make them:

- clear

- at the appropriate level of language. Teachers rarely teach the word *gap* or *suitable* to beginners, but they often use them in the test instructions. Remember to use the students' L1 if necessary. If not, you may be testing their instruction-reading skills instead of what you are actually trying to test.

Restrict the task

All the students should have the same chance. Look at the following compositions.

> **Computers**
>
> How can computers help us?
>
> How can computers help people at work?
>
> How can computers help the police, fire and ambulance services in emergencies?

Obviously the last task is the most restricted and will allow you to see differing ability better than the first. In addition, if you give a general topic and the student has no ideas, you are testing creativity as well as English.

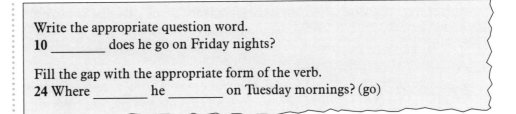 SEE CONSTRUCT VALIDITY (PAGE 19) They may need a fresh start (SEE PAGE 24).

Keep conditions comparable

Make sure two different groups take the test under the same conditions. The instructions must be the same. Do you pause the tape between plays? How long for? Is there distracting background noise? Can they cheat? Do you give them a minute to let them finish after *Time's up!*, or do you say *Pens down now!*?

TASK

Look at one of the end-of-year tests from your school. How reliable do you think it is? Think of at least one way of making it more reliable but taking the same amount of time.

"What is scorer reliability?" : SCORER RELIABILITY means *If you gave the same test to two different people to mark, would they give the same score?*

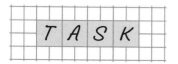

Look at the three answers to exercises below. What kind of test is each from? What kind of problems will you have when marking them for a) your class? b) another teacher's class?

> **Example 1:** 1 a   2 b   3 d   4 a   5 d
> **Example 2:** He ~~go~~ to the cinema.
> **Example 3:** Jonh get up and open de eyes. The sun is shinning and de brids are sinning. He tink, 'Is a beautiful day. Today, I no go to work, but I go to the beach.' But when he is driving in her car, he see Mr Smith, his boss, who say him, 'Why you not in work?'

Example 1: Multiple choice tests

It is easy to see that Example 1 is much easier to mark than Example 3. In fact, a computer can mark Example 1. But as we explained in CONTENT VALIDITY (PAGE 18), multiple-choice exams are much more difficult to write. And there are some skills – like writing – where testing by multiple-choice causes problems with validity. Another major drawback with multiple-choice exams is that the results don't help the student to learn. Neither teacher nor learner can get any useful information about **why** the learner's answer was right/wrong or successful/unsuccessful.

Example 2: Limited possibility tests

There are only a limited number of possible correct answers for Example 2. However, as we saw in CONSTRUCT VALIDITY (PAGE 19):

… there are often more possible answers than we anticipated when we wrote the question

… students can give answers which are partially correct and partially wrong.

"How can we improve scorer reliability in in these cases?" : Use an answer key or a marking guide: give a list of acceptable answers and a marking scheme (i.e. can you give half-marks? If so, what for?). But if more than one teacher is marking the tests, remember that you may need several meetings to add new acceptable answers to the list, or alter the marking scheme. For example, all the answers below are possible.

> **Ex. 2**   He _____ to the cinema.
> goes/went/will go/has been/will have gone/would like to go

Example 3: Multiple possibility tests

Example 3 is much more difficult to mark.

- Teacher A might notice that all the punctuation and present progressive forms are right.
- Teacher B might notice that all present simples are wrong and the spelling is terrible.
- Teacher C might think this is very creative and fluent.

- Teacher D might count 17 mistakes in 57 words (i.e. 30% wrong).
- Teacher E might say that this is a good essay for a beginner but bad for an intermediate student.

"How can we improve scorer reliability in these cases?"

You may need more than one teacher involved in the marking for two reasons: first, if more than one teacher is administering the exam, it is very important that all the teachers are marking it in the same way. Second, we are now judging the student's work rather than counting it, and even dancers are judged by a panel!

"How can we do this?"

The most important action is to negotiate and agree on the criteria you will all judge the answer by. This could be done by agreement on PROFILING (SEE PAGE 49): breaking down the answers you want into **either** their component parts, like spelling, punctuation, structure, cohesion; **or** other criteria, such as organisation, relevance, etc.; and/or BANDING (SEE PAGE 51): marking according to overall impression. We will return to this in a later chapter.

Some teachers will say that there is no time to have meetings or read documents to make sure they are marking the test in the same way as the other teachers. But if one teacher is marking the same test in a different way, everyone's time is wasted!

The results are simply not of any use, because the results are not comparable. So:

… the students have wasted their class time doing the test

… the teachers have wasted their time marking the test

… the school's administration has wasted its time recording the results

… the school is open to complaints from parents whose children will compare results on the way home: *I put the same thing as he did but he got it right and I got it wrong …*

Of all the qualities of a good test, SCORER RELIABILITY **is the only one that non-experts understand**. Ignoring SCORER RELIABILITY is a false economy!

Look at a current test used in your school. Are there clear and unambiguous marking instructions? How would you improve them?

Now try to answer all the questions as if you were the 'Student from Hell'!

Answer all the questions as unco-operatively as possible!

a Make sure that every answer you write is possible; but

b **either** not what the teacher actually wanted you to write (she was trying to test something else); **or** will cause the teacher other marking difficulties!

How would you change the test, but make it take the same amount of time?

Practicality

"What is practicality?"

Perhaps the most important quality of any test is how practical it is to administer. While we may want to have 1,000 questions, or give the students their own video-recorder for a listening test, we simply do not have the resources, that is, time, personnel, space, equipment or money.

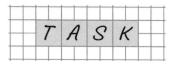

Read the following (idealised!) list of resources required for writing good tests. Which do your school have? Which could your school possibly arrange or get? Which are impossible for your school to arrange or get? What effect will this have on your school's testing system?

Time will be needed for:
teachers designing the test teachers analysing the results (e.g. how successful are the distractors, PAGE 36?) trialling it on sample groups teachers marking the papers students doing the test
Writing a test which is valid and reliable requires:
teachers who are experienced in test-writing teachers who are expert statisticians teachers to attend pre-marking standardisation sessions teachers to mark the tests co-ordinators to answer questions about alternative answers
Space and equipment
students need to be sitting where they can't copy (especially in multiple-choice tests) they may need different tables (e.g. one desk per person) teachers need good audio-/video tape-players with counters and pause/replay buttons they may need calculators or computers to record and analyse the results
Money for:
extra staff extra space extra equipment. (*However, this money is probably not available.*)

Backwash

"What is backwash?"

BACKWASH – sometimes called washback – refers to the effect that a final test has on the teaching programme that leads to it. This is a familiar experience, and is also sometimes called teaching to the test.

For example, the school SYLLABUS/objectives tell the teacher to teach fluency, but the school's final test is, e.g. a multiple-choice grammar and vocabulary test. Most teachers want their students to pass the test – possibly the teachers will have their teaching performance assessed on the basis of the students' success (or lack of it), therefore most teachers will teach grammar and vocabulary rather than fluency.

Sometimes the effect of this BACKWASH can improve the teaching programme: this is called beneficial BACKWASH. For example: the school management notices that students at the end of the teaching programme know their grammar but cannot speak the target language. They decide on radical action! They drop all grammar items in the test and instead introduce interviews on video by other teachers of the target language. Teachers therefore change their teaching to give more emphasis to the speaking skill.

We could also introduce a concept such as frontwash. This is the effect that new teaching techniques or materials have on the design of tests. For example, the introduction of communicative teaching methodology and materials has undoubtedly influenced or changed the content and emphasis of many local and international tests.

Can you think of any examples where you have changed your teaching in response to changes in the SYLLABUS?

Can you think of any examples where you have changed your teaching in response to changes in the assessment system (i.e., not the SYLLABUS)?

Can you think of any examples where the assessment system has been changed because you – or your coursebook – have changed your teaching style?

Summary

Given the resources we have, we will always have to make a compromise between how reliable a test is and how practical a test is. For this reason, we should use test results not to decide someone's abilities, but more as one factor in helping us to assess a student's performance. Test results guide, they do not dictate.

VALIDITY looks at whether your test tests what you want it to test. TEST RELIABILITY looks at whether your test results accurately reflect the student's performance.

Writing a valid and reliable test that gives results you can trust requires enormous resources. Often such a test is not practical as many of the resources required are probably not available. Although we will try hard to make the test as good as possible, we will probably not be able to trust in-house tests to make crucial decisions about students. Therefore we should use in-house test results as a guide, or only part of an overall student evaluation system.

We should also be aware of the BACKWASH effect – are we teaching the students something because it is in the exam or because they really need it to build their language knowledge?

CHAPTER 5

What forms of testing and evaluation should we use?

Direct and indirect testing

"What is direct testing?"

DIRECT TESTING means we ask the student to perform what we want to test.

"What is indirect testing?"

INDIRECT TESTING means we test things that give us an indication of the student's performance.

In DIRECT TESTING, we talk to students to see if they can communicate their ideas in interactive conversation. This sounds obvious, but it is not always practical to do this, e.g. a student may be away sick, or the class may be too big to speak to each member for enough time, especially if there is a strict SYLLABUS to adhere to.

In INDIRECT TESTING we would find things that give us an indication of how well the students can speak. For example, we know that good speakers use longer sentences or utterances than weak speakers. We could then invent a test where we measure skills associated with good speaking, e.g. the average length of each utterance: the longer the utterance, the higher the grade.

The same is true for writing. We could directly ask the students to write a number of texts. This would tell us about their writing skills. However, there may be reasons (e.g. restricted marking time) why we can't ask the students actually to perform this skill. Therefore we might give them a test on linker words (e.g. *however*, etc.). This may give us an indication of their ability to write well.

In the examples above, we are assuming a connection between length of utterance and speaking ability; and linkers and writing ability.

One problem is making sure that the INDIRECT TEST is an extremely good indicator or has a HIGH CORRELATION with the skill we are trying to test. If we find students who cannot write achieve high scores on our linkers test, this shows linkers are not a good indicator. This will make the test result invalid.

INDIRECT TESTING also often produces a negative BACKWASH effect (SEE PAGE 28): some teachers will spend hours in the classroom teaching linkers rather than teaching writing, because that's what is in the test.

These problems cannot exist when we use DIRECT TESTING methods. Therefore, whenever possible, use them.

DIRECT TESTS are preferable to INDIRECT TESTS. Some teachers would argue that, as language teachers, we are teaching students to communicate – in other words, to use language.

We use language in talking (speaking and listening), reading and writing. Someone can be good at grammar but unable to communicate in speech or writing. In this case, grammar, vocabulary and pronunciation tests must really all be forms of indirect testing.

So we should place more emphasis on results from skills tests than grammar and vocabulary tests.

Do you agree?

Do you think your school agrees?

How much of your students' final assessment is based on their ability to communicate – to use and experiment with the language they have learned? How much is based on their ability to manipulate grammar and vocabulary? Do you agree with this balance?

Norm-referenced and criteria-referenced testing

These terms refer to the way a test is made and the way the results of a test are presented.

"What is norm-referenced testing?"

When the results of the test compare a student with other students. The result does not give any information about individual performance, only a comparison with other students' performances – from that year and from other years.

For example, a university wants to restrict entry to its (science) courses to the applicants who have the best chance of successfully completing a course. In the past, it has found – perhaps by trial and error – that students who scored 80% or more in their final school year exams are the candidates most likely to succeed. Therefore they offer places only to students from your school who got 80% or 16/20 in their final science exams.

"What is criteria-referenced testing?"

When the result tells you about what the individual student can do, and does not compare him/her with other students. It describes certain criteria that the student has been able to meet.

For example, a student is applying for a job which requires the ability to use a word-processor. The employer does not want a computer expert, only someone who can do basic word-processing: typing; file-management; simple cut, copy and paste commands. The student takes a word-processing course and the final exam tests these skills.

The employer doesn't need to know if anyone else on the course was better or worse. He/she simply wants to know what the candidate can do.

"So which is better...?"

As we saw above, it is the state and large international examination boards who are most concerned with comparing people. The value of their qualifications depends upon year-on-year comparison and consistency. For example, many people feel that 'exams these days aren't as difficult as when I was at school'. Lack of year-on-year consistency devalues the state's awards, like university places and university degrees. However, this need for consistency means it is very difficult to improve or develop exams because results wouldn't be comparable.

There is a similarity here with DIRECT and INDIRECT TESTING. ◆ SEE PAGE 30

CRITERIA-REFERENCED TESTS can be directly interpreted by the user: an employer can read a description to discover what the student can do.

NORM-REFERENCED TESTS are not directly interpretable: you can only use the result by comparing one student's result with your past experience of other people with the same score.

For teachers and students, it is obviously more useful for us to know what a student can and cannot do so we can work on the areas where there are problems. However, the state and other large organisations need to reduce complexity – they want simple and consistent measurement.

Forms of evaluation

First we must remember the difference between simple testing and evaluation. In this book, the term *testing* is used when we are asking the students questions to which we already know the answers. We are using the term *evaluation* to ask the students questions to which we don't know the answers – genuine questions: *Do the students feel they are getting better? Have they found the course useful?*

We earlier identified several different types of test: PROFICIENCY TESTS, ACHIEVEMENT TESTS, PLACEMENT TESTS and DIAGNOSTIC TESTS (SEE PAGE 8). However, in all these tests, we are testing the students to see where they fit in to our system and our criteria. We are in control.

But evaluation is different because we are asking questions to learn about the student's learning process and attitudes, and about the teaching programme.

There are three common terms used when describing evaluation: SUMMATIVE, FORMATIVE and CONGRUENT EVALUATION.

"What is summative evaluation?" This is done at the end of (a stage of) a process. In teaching, this might be at the end of a term or a year. In this way, it is a kind of final assessment, summarising what has been achieved throughout that course. SUMMATIVE EVALUATION looks at general feedback to the teaching procedure used, so that next year's course can be changed according to what has been more or less successful.

"What is formative evaluation?" This is done during a process so that the process can be changed to make it more effective. In teaching, this might be feedback that a teacher gets to check how successful the teaching programme is. The feedback from the students can also affect the teaching procedure while there is still a chance to change it for the better – to help this year's students rather than next year's.

"What is congruent evaluation?" Less often referred to, this looks at the whole process before it starts, in order to make sure that the aims, methodology and evaluation of the course match the stated purpose and beliefs. For example, imagine your purpose is to increase the students' oral fluency. You ask teachers to design a course and a way to evaluate it. They return it to you and you notice that the tests include writing: this wouldn't match your original aims. In this way, CONGRUENT EVALUATION is very similar to CONTENT VALIDITY. ◆ SEE PAGE 18

Putting the three together

You will notice that there is, in effect, little difference between these terms, because evaluation never ends. SUMMATIVE EVALUATION at the end of a course informs the teacher – and students – about how to change the course next time to make it more successful and/or more closely related to the beliefs behind the course. SUMMATIVE EVALUATION will also have implications for the next course: if there are certain problem areas the following course will have to be changed to allow more (or less) time on these; or focus on different areas.

In other words, the difference between SUMMATIVE, FORMATIVE and CONGRUENT EVALUATION is not one of **how** evaluation is done, but **when** and **why** evaluation is done.

- CONGRUENT EVALUATION tries to keep the process on the desired course.
- FORMATIVE EVALUATION tries to alter the process while it is still going on.
- SUMMATIVE EVALUATION tries to assess the success of the completed process.

Summary

In this chapter we have covered the following.

- INDIRECT TESTS test abilities related to the skill we are interested in.
- DIRECT TESTS test the skill itself.
- NORM-REFERENCED exams compare one person's performance with many others.
- CRITERIA-REFERENCED exams describe what one person can do without comparing them with others.
- CONGRUENT, FORMATIVE and SUMMATIVE EVALUATION describe when evaluation is done: before, during, or after. But it is important to remember that evaluation is not linear, but cyclical. Each part informs the other.

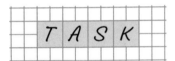

Think about when and why your school evaluates its students.

Does it ask the student genuine questions to improve the school's teaching:

a during the year or teaching programme?

b at the end of the year or teaching programme?

Does it ask you, the teacher, genuine questions to improve the school's teaching:

a during the year or teaching programme?

b at the end of the year or teaching programme?

Does your school examine new curricula, SYLLABUSES and assessment procedures before implementing them in order to check they match the school's aims?

Does your school's teaching programme have 'official' aims?

Why? Why not?

CHAPTER 6

Testing techniques for grammar and vocabulary

Once we have decided what we want to evaluate, we then have to design ways of getting data which allow us to make an assessment of students' abilities. One of the most common methods is giving tests. This section of the book will look at some different techniques that teachers often use in tests to get assessment data, and will assess their strengths and weaknesses.

Let's start by looking at how we can test single or discrete items: normally grammar or vocabulary items, or a combination of both. Note that some of these techniques can also be used to test passive skills, such as reading and listening. There is more on testing reading and listening in the next chapter.

We will look at five possible ways of testing for grammar and vocabulary:

1 Selection: true/false and multiple-choice questions

2 Gap-filling

3 Building sentences – recognition into production

4 Transformations and reformulations

5 Editing

1 Look at the following examples and match them with the five techniques above. The answers are in the following text.

> **a** Mr Brown normally _____ to the cinema on Tuesdays.
>
>   i) goes ii) comes iii) go iv) did go
>
> **b** Mr Brown normally _____ to the cinema on Tuesdays.
>
> **c** Mr Brown normally go to the cinema on Tuesdays. Right or wrong?
>
> **d** Mr Tuesdays cinema to on goes Brown normally the
>
> **e** Mr Brown / normally / go / cinema / Tuesdays
>
> **f** They made that car in Spain. That car _____ .
>
> **g** Mr Brown normally g_____ to t_____ cinema o_____ Tuesdays.

2 Now think of the language tests you use in your school.

Which of these techniques are the most commonly used for testing grammar?

Which of these techniques are the most commonly used for testing vocabulary? Why?

What problems have you and other teachers had using these techniques?

1 Testing techniques: True/false and multiple-choice questions

True/false and multiple-choice questions are probably the most popular testing technique found in tests today, largely because they are very easy to mark and have excellent SCORER RELIABILITY. ◆ SEE PAGE 25

However, they present several problems:

… they only test the student's ability to recognise a correct answer
… there may be problems in using true/false questions to test grammar
… there is a problem with students guessing the right answer
… they are extremely difficult to write
… sometimes they are impossible to write.

Let's look at these problems in more detail.

They only test the student's ability to recognise a correct answer

They do not test the student's ability to produce or use correct language, so it is often better to use them for testing passive skills (i.e. reading and listening). However, they are often also used for testing grammar and/or vocabulary. In this case, remember that you are testing the student's ability to **recognise** a correct form or word. You cannot assume that they can actually **produce** it.

There may be problems in using true/false questions to test grammar

We normally use true/false questions to test passive skills. If we use true/false-type questions to test grammar or vocabulary, we are essentially asking the students to mark the sentence right or wrong. Look at the following examples.

Testing vocabulary

		T	F
Text:	Mr Brown often sees a film at the weekends.		
Q:	He normally goes to the cinema on Tuesdays.	☐	☐

Note: This is testing (recognition of) the word *weekends*.

Testing whether grammar is right or wrong

1 Is this sentence right (✓) or wrong (✗)?
Mr Brown normally go to the cinema on Tuesdays. ☐

2 Mark which sentence is correct (✓) :
a Mr Brown normally go to the cinema on Tuesdays. ☐
b Mr Brown normally goes to the cinema on Tuesdays. ☐

There is a problem with students guessing the right answer

By definition, true/false questions mean that the student has a 50% chance of a correct answer by guessing. This means that, if you want to have a pass mark, it would need to be much more than 50% to eliminate chance.

An alternative is to deduct marks for wrong answers. But what is the meaning of the final mark you give? The wrong answers may be the result of imperfect understanding, while the correct answers may be the result of guessing.

So far, we have looked at true/false questions, where the student has a one-or-the-other alternative. The obvious way of reducing the chances of passing by guessing is to give more than one alternative answer, as in multiple-choice questions, e.g.

Mr Brown normally _____ to the cinema on Tuesdays.

a) goes   **b) arrives**   **c) go**   **d) did go**

There is normally only one correct possibility. The alternative (wrong) answers are called *distractors*, and there are normally between three and five possibilities.

They are extremely difficult to write

The biggest problem is creating wrong alternative answers that look possible. In the example above, would it be legitimate to use grammatically wrong alternatives, e.g. *wented*? Many teachers feel unhappy about presenting their students with incorrect language in case they somehow 'learn' it.

Because we want the test to 'look nice', we tend to use the same number of distractors for each test item. However, there are often not three or more viable alternatives. Thus we have to use a distractor that clearly doesn't fit, e.g. *arrives*. This means that really the student has to make a choice of one out of three, rather than one out of four. The distractors that we do use can often show the student the correct answer, e.g. *arrives* may remind the student that a final *-s* is required.

It is almost impossible to write distractors that are not somehow correct in certain circumstances, and this can often lead to arguments with students about the context. This problem can be avoided in reading or listening texts by supplying a context, but this is more difficult to do when testing context-free grammar or vocabulary items. For example, this is a possible sentence in English, with this stress pattern:

Mr Brown normally did go to the cinema on Tuesdays.

Sometimes true/false or multiple-choice questions are impossible to write

Only certain areas of language learning can be tested by multiple-choice, e.g. it is very difficult to test writing or speaking in this way. But because multiple-choice questions are so apparently easy to write and mark, they get used more and more. Teachers may then start writing tests which avoid areas of language that are not easily tested in this way, and, because of the BACKWASH effect (SEE PAGE 28), such areas often won't get taught.

2 Testing techniques: Gap-filling

Whereas true/false and multiple-choice questions test recognition, gap-filling questions test production. There are three considerations with gap-filling-type questions.

"Should we give a context or not?"

Context here means *Do we put the language in its natural environment, or do we use, for example, only single sentences?*

For testing specific grammar or vocabulary items, context is sometimes omitted:

> Mr Brown normally _____ to the cinema on Tuesdays.
>
> You see films at the _____.

This may cause problems as we have seen above, because more than one answer may be possible.

Gap-fills are often used in longer texts:

> On a typical day, Mr Brown *gets* up at 7.00 am. He _____ dressed and then _____ downstairs and _____ his breakfast. Then he _____ to work in his car. He _____ lunch at 1.00 p.m. He _____ home at 5.00 p.m. and, after _____ his dinner, _____ television until midnight, when he _____ to bed.

At higher levels, or with longer texts, there are normally no gaps in the first twenty words or paragraph. This is to orientate the student in the context. When we are more interested in testing grammar, we often answer the first question to give a guide to the kind of answer we want.

However, in the gap-fill above we have reminded the student that the third person -s exists, and so the rest of the test may simply be testing vocabulary.

"Should we give a guide as to what to put in the gap or not?"

This raises the question of how much, if any, help we should give the student. Apart from a sample answer, the examples above gave the student no assistance. But we **can** give the student a certain amount of help as to what goes in the gap.

> Mr Brown normally _____ to the cinema on Tuesdays. (go)
>
> You see films at the c_____.
>
> On a typical day, Mr Brown _____ at   get up
>
> 7.00 am. He _____ dressed and then   get
>
> _____ downstairs and _____ his   go/have
>
> breakfast.

When to give assistance depends on three testing problems.

- When we are testing the student's ability to transform something (e.g. the infinitive into the third person -s; an active to passive, etc.).
- When we want to force the student to use a desired item.
- When we want to put the same idea in each student's head, to avoid testing originality, or to avoid testing vocabulary when we are more interested in structure, for example.

 But ... notice that forcing the student to use an item is often the sign of a bad test: sometimes any word will fit in the gap, so we have to limit the student because we can't write a good enough question. It is the result of a SCORER RELIABILITY problem. ◆ SEE PAGE 26

"Should we choose specific items to be gapped or not?"

In the text above, the teacher has decided which words should be omitted. However, an alternative is a cloze test, where words are deleted not according to what we want to test, but on a regular basis.

> On a typical day, Mr Brown gets up at 7.00 a.m. He gets dressed _____
> then goes downstairs and has his _____. Then he drives to work in
> _____ car. He has lunch at 1.00 p.m. _____ drives home at 5.00 p.m.
> and, after _____ dinner, watches television until midnight, when _____
> goes to bed.

In this example, every seventh word has been deleted (except the first, in order to give context). This is obviously testing a different skill from the previous gapped text. The theory is that any native speaker can easily predict the word that fills the gap. It tests the student's understanding of the whole language.

It also assumes that elementary students only know a simplified version of the language, so it is important to use a text at the student's level of understanding.

However, most teachers change this pure cloze idea, and normally omit **approximately** every seventh word, making it a combination of a gapped text and a cloze text. Sometimes this is to test a particular item (e.g. a possessive pronoun, like *his*) and sometimes because the word is unguessable (e.g. *5.00 p.m.*). Most people therefore use between every seventh to every tenth word.

A variation on this is the C-test.

> On a typical day, Mr Brown gets up at 7.00 a.m. He gets dressed a_____ then
> g_____ downstairs a_____ has h_____ breakfast. T_____ he d_____ to
> w_____ in h_____ car. H_____ has l_____ at 1.00 p.m. H_____ drives
> h_____ at 5.00 p.m. a_____, after e_____ dinner, w_____ television
> u_____ midnight, w_____ he g_____ to b_____ .

After setting the context, every second word is deleted but the first letter is given. It has the advantage for the teacher that many more questions can be asked in a much shorter space. Once again, you have to make decisions about how to treat unguessable words (names, times, etc.). Remember that this is a language exercise and not a test of students' intellect! Remember also that the text must be at the students' level.

Find a text that you can give to your students (at least two paragraphs), and make two copies. Make sure it is at their level.

From one copy make a cloze test and count the number of gaps. Then make a C-test from the other copy but keeping the number of gaps the same as in the cloze test, e.g. use just the first paragraph.

Divide the class into two groups. Give Group A the cloze version of the whole text. Give Group B the C-test version. Mark their answers. Any surprises?

3 Testing techniques: Building sentences – recognition into production

When we want to test students' abilities to build sentences, we have the same decisions to make about how much we want to help them, and whether to give them some context.

The simplest level is one of recognition with maximum help. We can do this by using a jumbled sentence.

| Mr | Tuesdays | cinema | to | on | goes | Brown | normally | the |

Answer: Mr Brown normally goes to the cinema on Tuesdays.

Of course, we have to accept other possibilities, such as:

On Tuesdays Mr Brown normally goes to the cinema.

Capital letters sometimes tell the student which is the first word. If you have only one capital letter in the sentence, do you give it a mark (the student has recognised the purpose of the punctuation) or not allocate the first word a mark? Whichever you decide, make sure all the markers/teachers agree!

Be careful with punctuation, e.g.

| Mr | Tuesdays | . | cinema | to | on | goes | Brown | normally | the |

The teacher has included the full-stop to show the student the last word. But how do the students know whether the full-stop is attached to *Tuesday*, or just another element to put in order?

The next level of complexity is slashed sentences or note expansion. These ask the students to produce correct language rather than just recognise it, by omitting function words such as pronouns and prepositions.

| Mr Brown / normally / go / cinema / Tuesdays |

Note that it is possible to use units longer than a single sentence, by slashing a sequence of sentences.

Context can be added by using different text types, e.g.

> Dear Sally
>
> I / sorry / I / (not write) / for ages. I / (just come back) / holiday in Turkey.

In this example, we have put verbs or words that the students might need to alter in brackets. Otherwise the students might think they have to use the words as they stand. You need to make this clear in the instructions. (Remember you can use the student's L1 for instructions.)

> Expand the sentences, keeping the words in the same order.
> You may need to add words or change the form of words in brackets.
>
> Mr Brown / normally / (go) / cinema / Tuesdays.

4 Testing techniques: Transformations and reformulations

Another method of holistic testing – that is, not just testing linguistic components but a general ability in the target language – is to see if students can take a sentence/meaning and express it in a different way. In other words, can they express the same idea but using different linguistic items?

> Complete the sentences so that the meaning is as close as possible to the original.
>
> He's a doctor. He works *as a doctor*.
>
> They made that car in Spain. That car *was made* in Spain.

In this example, the students are given part of the sentence, which they have to complete. Note that it doesn't need to be the beginning of the sentence.

Another possibility is to give the students a word or phrase to use in the transformed sentence, e.g.

> Rewrite the sentences using the given word. Keep the meaning as close as possible to the original.
>
> He's a doctor.
>
> _____. works
>
> They made that car in Spain.
>
> _____. was

The instructions (which may be in the L1) are very important in these exercises: the students must keep the sentence as close as possible in meaning to the original sentence. If they don't understand this, you will have many SCORER RELIABILITY problems (SEE PAGE 26) as students will give answers which are acceptable English but use different ideas, e.g.

> He works *in a hospital*. That car *was* made in Spain by them.

So we can see that the major problems will be:

… avoidance of the target test item (*works as*), or

… redundant information (*by them*) included in the answer.

Apart from these, a further problem with this exercise type is that there are relatively few items that can be tested using this method. The most common tend to be:

reported speech	'Go away!' he said.	He told …
passives	They made that car in Spain.	That car …
too/enough	They're too young to go to the disco.	They're not …
comparatives/superlatives	I have never seen such a big cake.	It was …
modals	It isn't necessary to reserve a room.	You …
conditionals	You won't pass if you don't study.	Unless …
since/for	She's been driving since 1993.	… for …

You will notice that most of these are more frequently tested at intermediate or upper intermediate level. You will also notice that these are also the items most frequently taught at those levels. A perfect example of BACKWASH?

5 Testing techniques: Editing

Editing is increasingly used in modern tests. The idea is to find mistakes (or a lack of mistakes) in a text.

> Read the following letter, and mark each line as right or wrong.
>
> Dear Susie,
> I'm sorry I haven't written for ages,   ✓
> but I hope I see you next week.   —
> That's because I'm having party.   —
> It'll be on Saturday afternoon at 3 o'clock on my flat.   —

Notice that in this example students simply have to choose right or wrong. Many exams now also ask for a correction, e.g.

> Read the following letter, and mark each line as right (✓) or wrong (✗). If the answer is wrong, write either the correct form or the missing word.
> Show where the word is missing by inserting a double slash (//).
>
> Dear Susie,
> I'm sorry I haven't written for ages,   ✓   ____
> but I hope I // see you next week.   ✗   'll
> That's because I'm having party.   —   ____
> It'll be on Saturday afternoon at 3 o'clock on my flat.   —   ____

"What is the value of this exercise?"

Every mistake you find in a student's work is a mistake they haven't found themselves. We all want students to become more responsible for their learning. This may even be part of their assessment.

An essential part of this responsibility is for each student to look at his/her work critically, and these exercises are one of the best ways of encouraging this process.

There is a sample editing task on PHOTOCOPIABLE PAGE 2 for you to try with your students. You could do this to familiarise your students with the exercise type before doing the task below.

This kind of exercise is a very easy one for students to write.

Ask groups of students to write a similar letter made up of short sentences. Ask them to put in between four and six mistakes, each one in a different sentence. They then rewrite it, putting each sentence on a different line and pass it to the next group, who corrects the sentences. At the end of the class, collect the best texts or individual sentences.

Note: Don't make them all put the same number of mistakes, or they will simply be looking for, say, five mistakes.

Summary

	Recognise	Produce

Specific item	– true/false
	– multiple choice
	– editing skills
	  (without correction)
		– gap fill
		– transformation/reformulation
		– editing skills
		  (with correction)

General ability		– cloze test – C-test

Discrete item tests: error hunt

Look at one of the books you are currently using. No book or printed text is ever perfect (including this one!), and writers often have a preference for one type of exercise.

Try to find examples of the following.

a a multiple-choice grammar question where more than one of the distractors is possible!

b a multiple-choice question where you can answer the question without reading the text

c a multiple-choice exercise which has a varying number of distractors (e.g. sometimes three, sometimes four)

d a pure cloze test (i.e. one where every nth word has been cut out, rather than a grammar test where just the difficult words have been omitted)

e a transformation exercise that can have more than one answer

f a jumbled sentence which can be put in two different orders

g a gap-filling exercise where the writer tells you if contractions (e.g. *don't*) count as one word or two words

CHAPTER 7

Testing techniques for reading and listening

So far we have mainly concentrated on testing single words/structures or single sentences. We have looked at techniques where you:

… select or match an answer from two or more options (e.g. true/false and multiple-choice)

… order words to form a sentence

… expand given words or notes into a sentence

… transform the same idea into a different form of expression

… fill a space (possibly guided by suggestions, which is then similar to multiple choice).

However, many of these same ideas can be used to test longer pieces of language through reading or listening.

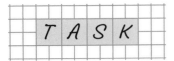

Can you think of how these techniques are normally adapted for dealing with longer listening/reading texts? Which techniques would be better for reading? Which would be better for listening? Why?

General points: Reading and listening

Many techniques for testing listening can also be used for testing reading. But not all the techniques for testing reading can be used for listening. This is because, with longer texts, listening requires students to retain a lot of information in their heads – you will be testing their memory rather than their listening ability. Listening texts that require memory should be very short.

If you want to use longer listening texts, the students' task will have to be something that they can do during the listening: (short) multiple-choice questions, marking a diagram, following a map, etc.

It is essential with multiple-choice listening tests that you do not deliberately confuse the student, e.g. multiple-choice questions should be in the same order as the text, and not mixed up to trick the student.

Remember that students may get lost. If they miss an answer, they may still be listening for it while the tape has moved on. In other words, by missing one answer, they often miss several following answers. For this reason, it is normally a good idea to use a number of smaller texts with clear starts and finishes. This also gives the student a fresh start. ◆ SEE PAGE 24

1 Selection

While the students are reading/listening to the text, or after they have read/ listened to it, they select one right answer from two or more possibilities, e.g.

> Listen to the text, and choose which person the man is describing.
>
> Listen to the text, and draw the route they take on the map.
>
> Read the letter, and choose which of the four letters is the best answer to it.
>
> Read the information about the family, and choose which holiday best suits them.

There are thousands of possible ways of using selection. However, the best ways will be the ones that match real life. For example, we read reviews of computer games before we buy one or we choose a pen-friend from a selection of letters. Few, if any, people read all the horoscopes to select their ideal star-sign (often the type of exercise given in tests/books).

2 Matching

While the students are reading or listening to the text, or after they have read or listened to it, they match one right answer from two or more possibilities, e.g.

---

1 Here are five newspaper articles (1 – 5), and five headlines (A – E). Which headline belongs to which article?

   1 __   2 __   3 __   4 __   5 __

2 Here are five letters 1 – 5, and five answers to them, marked A – E. Read them and decide which answer matches which letter.

   1 __   2 __   3 __   4 __   5 __

3 Read the following article. You will notice that five paragraphs have been removed (1 – 5). At the end of the article you will find five paragraphs (A – E). Which paragraph goes in which space?

   1 __   2 __   3 __   4 __   5 __

There are ways in which we can complicate the student's task, if we want to.

Distractors

We can include information which does not have a match, e.g.

Here are five newspaper articles (1 – 5), and six headlines (A – F). Which headline belongs to which article?

   1 __   2 __   3 __   4 __   5 __

Note: Of course, we could give ten headlines.

Alternatively, we could ask the following question.

Here are five newspaper articles (1 – 5), and six headlines (A – F). Which headline does not belong to any article? __

Multiple matching

Multiple matching means that more than one answer is possible. There does not have to be a one-to-one match. There could be one-to-many matches, or many-to-one matches.

Here are five answers from a youth magazine's problem page (A–E). Below are eight letters sent in by the readers (1–8). Which answer(s) would be appropriate for which problems.

Note: sometimes more than one answer is possible.

1 _ _ _   2 _ _ _   3 _ _ _   4 _ _ _

5 _ _ _   6 _ _ _   7 _ _ _   8 _ _ _

TIP

We automatically send a signal by the number of spaces we put for each question. The above example suggests that there are three possible answers for each. You can give the students additional help by only putting the correct number of spaces.

Problems with matching exercises

Matching exercises all share the same problem, which is that if the students make one wrong match, they must, by definition also get another answer wrong. This can be an even bigger problem when setting multiple-matching exercises. You may need to have meetings to agree on pass marks: if you ask five questions, for example, one mistake will mean the student gets only three out of five correct (i.e. 60% – a wrong answer loses 40% of the mark!).

As we saw with true/false and multiple-choice questions, you may decide to penalise wrong answers, but the resulting mark then doesn't mean anything. However you decide to treat error, it is important that the markers all agree on whether or how to penalise such mistakes.

3 Ordering

Once again, this device can be used for longer pieces of text. Because of the mental load, this is probably best reserved for reading rather than listening.

Note: Giving the opening and closing paragraphs helps to give context.

Below you will find the opening and closing paragraphs of a personal letter.
You will also see five paragraphs (A – E) that go in the letter.
Read the paragraphs and decide which order they go in.

1st __   2nd __   3rd __   4th __   5th __

Below you will find five newspaper articles (A – E).
Read the articles and decide which order they go in.

1st __   2nd __   3rd __   4th __   5th __

Note: The same marking problem exists as with matching: if one answer is wrong, then at least two answers are. A correct answer will depend on the right sequence. For example, imagine the correct answer is:

1st A	**2nd** B	**3rd** C	**4th** D	**5th** E

and the student writes:

1st A	**2nd** B	**3rd** D	**4th** E	**5th** C

How many mistakes has the student made? If we mark by sight, i.e. as a computer would, only two answers (A and B) are in the correct position. However, the student has also identified that E follows D. Like matching, one mistake means that the student only gets three out of five correct and, again, you may need to have meetings to agree on pass marks.

4 Transforming the same idea into a different form of expression

This is obviously a test of language production, and therefore will be best used for testing speaking or writing. The idea is to keep one variable (e.g. the idea, or the text-type) the same, while changing another variable (e.g. the social style or level of formality).

> You are having a party and you are sending out the printed invitation below. You decide it is too formal to send to your best friend. Using the information on the invitation, finish this letter inviting her. (50 words)
>
> Dear Susie,
>
> I'm sorry I haven't written for ages, but I hope I'll see you next week ...

5 Filling a space

This could be possibly guided by suggestions, which is then similar to multiple-choice or to expanding given words or notes into a sentence.

One of the most familiar forms of testing longer texts is the open question, e.g.

> Why did John decide to buy the book?

We can help the student by guiding them to an answer, e.g.

> Why did John decide to buy the book?
>
> Because it reminded him of _____

Or, of course, we could use simple multiple-choice questions, e.g.

> Why did John decide to buy the book? Because it ...
> a) was cheap.
> b) reminded him of a book he had when he was younger.
> c) was the right size.
> d) looked interesting.

When testing longer texts, all the usual problems with multiple-choice still apply, e.g. the complexity of the distractors, more than one possible answer in context, etc. The most common problem (or solution, if you are a student!) is that the longest option is often the right one.

Another way of guiding the student to the answer is to ask them to expand given words or notes into a text. We have already seen how several sentences can be linked in context to use this device for longer pieces of text. However, you can also use it for longer pieces of writing to put the same ideas into everyone's heads, as we saw in TEST RELIABILITY (PAGE 22), e.g.

> Below you will find the opening and closing paragraphs of a personal letter.
> You will see that the middle paragraph is missing.
> Write the missing paragraph, including the following information:
> – you are visiting her town next month (why?)
> – you would like to stay (when? how long?)
> – you will be accompanied by a friend (who? why?)
> – your friend has a special diet (what? why?)

Summary

	Recognise	Produce
Specific item	– true/false – multiple choice – selection – matching – ordering	– gap-filling – note expansion – transformation/reformulation
General ability	◆ SEE CHAPTER 8	= writing and speaking ◆ SEE CHAPTER 9

If we want to test students' ability to understand longer texts, we must decide if we want them to understand particular items in the text, or the idea behind the text. If your answers depend on particular structural forms or individual pieces of vocabulary, remember you are actually testing single items, and not the students' ability to deal with long text.

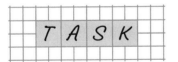

Look at a typical skills test from your school.

How many questions test reading and listening skills (skimming, listening for gist, etc.)? How many fresh starts (PAGE 24) does a student get in:

a) the reading section?   b) the listening section?

How many different text-types (newspapers, letters, posters, signs, etc.) does the student read? How many different text-types (news, songs, chat-shows, etc.) does the student listen to or look at?

How many different techniques do the students use in the test?

Is the test fair? Does it test the skills or do 'hidden' grammar/vocabulary questions also appear?

CHAPTER 8

Testing techniques with no correct answers

Sometimes we may not want to restrict the number of possible answers as there may well be many different and correct possibilities; and scorers may mark these in different ways. This type of question can be used as a teaching device, or a prompt for asking the students what they think and why. This takes us into the world of ILLUMINATION and evaluation, rather than ENUMERATION and testing.

1 Choosing a title

In this type of question, the student reads a text and then suggests a good title, or illustration, or some other way of showing their understanding of the text as a whole, e.g.

> Read the description of winter below. Imagine you are a publisher. Which of the four photos would you choose to illustrate this text? Why?

2 Ranking and ordering preferences

This relates to the student's personal beliefs, e.g.

> Read the following four descriptions (A – D) of the photograph.
>
> Which one describes it best? Put the paragraphs in order of preference.
>
> **1** (best) ___ **2** ___ **3** ___ **4** (worst) ___

There can obviously be no correct answer (although you may have a hidden agenda to make students aware of good writing). You can extend this question by asking *Explain why you think it is the best/worst description.*

3 Personalisation

You can also use personalisation, which will mean that answers will be different for each different student, e.g.

> Read the four advertisements for multi-media computers.
> Which do you find the most persuasive for your family's needs? Why?

Summary

Students can, for example, read a text and show their understanding by justifying their answers. Remember, however, not to mark these answers for grammatical accuracy or closeness to your opinion, as this is not what you are testing.

Look at the TV guide on PHOTOCOPIABLE PAGE 3. Devise a short reading task around it, which has no correct answer. Compare your ideas with those on PAGE 95.

PART C **Assessment**

CHAPTER 9

Assessing speaking and writing

So far, the majority of the techniques we have seen have been mainly ones where we turn the student's abilities into something we can count. However, we should remember that there are some abilities that cannot be counted, and therefore must be judged. Assessment can and should be used to help the students to learn as well simply to test them. By showing the students how we assess, they develop the criteria to evaluate their own work.

We will now look at forms of assessment which try to include students in the judging of their work.

Profiling and analytic marking schemes

As we saw in SCORER RELIABILITY (SEE PAGE 26), one major difficulty in evaluating language use is eliminating scorer subjectivity. Many teachers mark oral and written work by impression: they read it without concentrating on any particular part such as grammar, and instead give it a grade based on the general effect of the composition or speaking.

However, as we have seen on PAGE 26, different teachers may notice different things. So assessors have looked for a way of helping them standardise their marking.

One idea to make scoring more reliable is to break down an overall impression mark into a number of sub-skills. In this way, we can punish, say, spelling errors, while rewarding accuracy in grammar. Some of these sub-skills may be linguistic (structures, vocabulary, etc.), but others may not be (relevance, hand-writing, etc.).

T A S K

You are trying to assess a piece of written work.

Which of the areas in the chart on the next page do you think are linguistic, and which are non-linguistic, that is, which could be judged by a student as well as a teacher? Complete the chart.

	Teacher only	Teacher and student
handwriting		
appropriate social style		
layout		
organisation		
interest		
spelling		
a convincing argument		
range of vocabulary		
relevance to the task set or title		
use of linking words		
punctuation		
paragraphing		
accuracy of tenses		
use of rhetorical devices		
ideas easy to understand		

Analytic marking schemes

...and that was how enture ended.

Relevance	4
Adequacy	3
Grammar	1
Vocabulary	2
Punctuation	4
Total:	**14/25**

Both PROFILES and ANALYTIC MARKING SCHEMES try to break down communication into a number of different areas so that both teacher and student can see where they are successful and where the reader/listener has difficulties in understanding. Examples of such areas are grammar, vocabulary, relevance, punctuation, adequacy, and so on.

In this book, we will make a distinction between marking schemes and PROFILES. We will define a marking scheme as where you just have an impression mark for each area, marked, e.g. out of 5. So a student might get the mark on the left at the end of a composition.

While this score is less subjective, the student has no definition of what the teacher means, for example, by 'adequacy'.

Profiling

We want to give the students more information, such as where their problem areas are or how to improve. This means you can discuss the problem together knowing that you mean the same thing, or that a student can re-read the composition thinking of how to improve this one area.

A PROFILE, then, is not so much a score. It is more like a reference to a description of the person's ability – a description which is given to the student. The technical term for each of these descriptions is a DESCRIPTOR. There are normally between three and five levels. An example for using vocabulary in speech/writing might be:

```
3 Complete understanding with appropriate vocabulary
  and few, if any, circumlocutions
2 Meaning understood despite occasional inappropriate
  vocabulary or circumlocutions
1 Meaning not fully clear or ambiguous because of
  restricted/inappropriate vocabulary
0 Vocabulary so restricted that the meaning cannot be
  understood
```

it was Lucy who
race after all.

Relevance	3
Adequacy	2
Grammar	2
Vocabulary	3
Punctuation	2
Total:	12/15

This could be given to the student in both L1 and the target language (after all, it is authentic-to-the-classroom language), but you might want to simplify the language or concepts as appropriate. Thus a student's essay might be given the PROFILE on the left.

Note that here, the 'total' is simply an artificial device for record-keeping and/or diagnosis. What is more useful is that the students can look at the DESCRIPTORS, see in general terms what their problems are, and then discuss them with the teacher asking, e.g. for specific examples where the teacher found the use of vocabulary inadequate. Once students are familiar with the process and the vocabulary, older students can perhaps, after some practice sessions, start to discuss each other's compositions. This is an example of assessment that teaches.

Banding

BANDING is similar to PROFILING, but we will define it in this book as where the numbers or grades assigned point to DESCRIPTORS and relate to levels of ability. For each skill, there are normally nine or ten bands, representing approximately 100 hours of tuition each. So, for example, Speaking Band 1 will normally be:

```
Band 1
Cannot speak in the target language or, at least,
gives this impression.
```

whereas Band 10 will be:

```
Native speaker level: reacts appropriately to
unpredictable input in real time.
```

Between Band 1 and Band 10 will be other descriptions that cover the range of abilities between complete beginner and native speaker.

A BAND describes an ability level in any one skill, and therefore a writing BAND, for example, would include information concerning relevance, adequacy, grammar, vocabulary and punctuation at different levels. It is like a 'global' PROFILE.

"How would we use bands?"

The student would hand us a composition, for example. We would read it and hand it back to the student with the comment: *Band 3*. The student would then refer to a copy of the BANDS and read the following (in L1 and/or English):

```
Band 3
The reader can see that the writer has tried to
organise their writing to help understanding, but
this is either done very simply or, where more
complex organisation is attempted, the reader may
need to re-read parts several times before fully
understanding the connections and distinctions. There
are frequent inappropriacies, inaccuracies, or
circumlocutions in vocabulary and/or grammar, but the
overall idea is still clear.
```

We could then encourage the student to find examples of circumlocutions, or the student could try and prove to us that the essay was really a Band 4.

These kinds of BANDS and DESCRIPTORS are designed to cover linguistic ability ranging from complete beginners to near-native speaker in approximately nine or ten steps. A jump from one BAND to another, e.g. from Band 3 to Band 4, may therefore represent a jump of 100 hours or a whole academic year. However, teachers can show progress during the year through using half-bands, like 3+, 3/4 and 4-.

TIP

BANDS are extremely useful to parents and other teachers because they describe what the student is generally able to do in the target language: a good example of CRITERIA REFERENCING. ◆ SEE PAGE 31

However, some students will not have a flat PROFILE – in other words, some of their (writing) sub-skills might be Band 2 (e.g. grammatical accuracy), and other sub-skills might be Band 5 (e.g. relevance to the task set, interest, organisation, etc.). In these cases, using PROFILES of different sub-skills will be more helpful for teachers, students and parents.

Problems with profiles and bands

PROFILES and BANDS try to standardise – and make comprehensible – the criteria we use to judge a piece of student's work. We are trying to make the subjective as objective as possible. Remember that SCORER RELIABILITY (SEE PAGE 26) is very important as it is the easiest area for students and parents to (mis!)understand.

Consequently, once more than one teacher is involved in giving scores, the system will only work if there is discussion, training and negotiation to define the meanings of the terms used and moderate teachers' scores.

Such moderation is best done by groups of teachers looking at or listening to sample work and discussing their assessments. For example, if you have several language teachers in your school, you can have a short meeting to discuss what scores you gave, and why. If you notice that you constantly give, say, a BAND one higher than everyone else, you will in future have to reduce your BANDING by 1, even if this hurts!

Ideally, each teacher should read/listen to the student's work once for each PROFILE: once for an adequacy score, once for a grammar score, etc. If possible, several teachers should read/listen to each piece of student's work so that they can standardise their scores. However, the general theory is that, once you have had moderation sessions, any four trained people will give the same range of results as any other four people.

Once you have these PROFILES, you can use them for all the language teaching in your school – including the students' mother tongue.

Of course, practicality will say that you won't have the time or resources for each teacher to assess each piece of work, but the principle of moderation is still essential if the scheme is to work across teachers and/or a school.

"How often should we have moderation sessions?"

You don't need to have continual moderation meetings. For example, at the start of the school year, you should have a couple of meetings and look at the work of a few good, average and weak students. You should agree among each other which BAND is appropriate for each piece of work.

Once you have done this, you can then use the BANDS for every piece of (written) work for every student in the school for the whole year (although a couple of extra moderation sessions during the year will, of course, improve consistency).

The advantages are obvious: if all the teachers are using the same marking scheme and (roughly) the same criteria, your couple of moderation sessions have been an excellent investment! Students moving between years or between teachers should no longer be a problem. PROFILES and BANDS can and should be sent to parents who will see that there is a coherent and principled system of evaluation in the school.

"How do you create your own profiles/bands?"

Many books and exam boards already have PROFILES that you can use for your class. Alternatively, you could write your own individual ones for your own class, or all the language teachers in the school – including the teachers of the L1 – could get together to write one set for the school; or you could write them with your class – this will give them good practice in writing and give them a stake in the descriptions. This will also encourage them to mark each other's work.

Example 1: Writing a set of general profiles for the whole school

Step 1

Decide on the 'Crunch Point': the most critical or important point of assessment. In some schools, this will be at the end of schooling when the students leave. Alternatively, it may be a problem year within the school, where results are consistently disappointing.

Step 2

Discuss and decide on the main problems the students are having at the Crunch Point: writing essays/letters, speaking, individual points of grammar, etc.

Step 3

Write DESCRIPTORS and/or PROFILES that describe what the perfect student can do at the Crunch Point. Check that these DESCRIPTORS cover the problems you identified at Step 2.

Step 4

Write DESCRIPTORS that describe what a new student into the school can do. This will probably be very little or nothing.

Avoid using subjective words like *satisfactory* (to whom?) or *adequate* (to what purpose?).

Step 5

Decide how many way-stages you want: 0–3 or 0–5. You should always have an even number (i.e. 0–3 = 4 stages), otherwise teachers and students will choose the middle one because it is cautious.

Four stages probably means better SCORER RELIABILITY and different teachers will be more likely to give the same result (because there are fewer to choose from).

Six stages means you can show greater student progress. It is more motivating for students to see movement than being stuck on the same score for a year or more.

Step 6

Each teacher brings samples of students' work – probably writing or a video of the class speaking – and chooses students who are typical at each level. A group of teachers assess the students using the PROFILES and see if they agree with each other. The PROFILES reflect what the school is trying to teach and the purpose of the assessment (CONGRUENT EVALUATION).

Example of a profile template

Most PROFILES will have a similar structure, although different nationalities, school subjects and ages will need to adapt them to fit their local situation.

```
3 Meaning completely understood with insignificant
  mistakes
2 Meaning understood despite some occasional
  difficulties
1 Meaning not fully clear and/or ambiguous because of
  errors. Reader needs to re-read or ask for
  clarification and/or further explanation
0 Meaning unclear. No evidence that the student can
  use or understand the target language
```

With a 0–5 scale, the top and bottom descriptors will remain the same, but you now have Scales 1–4 to add shades of grey and intermediate skill points. These additional scales can be useful and should include specific areas of difficulty you identified at Step 2. This then raises the students' awareness of the importance of these points, and hopefully, through BACKWASH (SEE PAGE 28), will lead to better teaching and learning.

Note: This will only happen if the students have copies of the PROFILES so that they can see where they are (un)successful.

Example 2: Writing a set of specific profiles

You could also write a set of specific profiles to try to solve problems at a micro-level, such as writing at intermediate level. They could even address individual tasks, like *Writing personal letters at intermediate level*. Once a problem like this becomes apparent:

… decide on the key indicators: these will be the most common problems students have at this level with this task

… try to group these problems, e.g. problems with layout; problems with grammar, etc.

… write each group in a list, ranked according to your assessment of difficulty

… divide your list into four or six horizontal DESCRIPTORS for use as PROFILING.

Advantages of profiling

Diagnostic/teaching

Using PROFILES actually allows the students to see where they need to improve their work. If a teacher writes *Good, a big improvement* on the bottom of their essays, for example, students do not know how they have improved. On the other hand, with PROFILES you can sit down with a student and explain where you had a problem and where he/she was successful.

Of course, the student can then try and prove to you by pointing to examples, places in the essay, where he/she has achieved the level. In this way, evaluation becomes a shared responsibility, or a process of negotiation. Students will begin to learn how to evaluate other students' essays and, more importantly, learn how to edit their own work before giving it in to mark.

TIP

Ask the students to mark their work using the PROFILES before handing it in. This is a variation on CONFIDENCE RATINGS. (SEE PAGE 59) I suspect that most teachers think that discussing this with the students is going to be very difficult. It need not be.

Profiling and oral skills

Notes, bands and scores from observing the student in class

The teacher should not always be involved in the activities going on in class. Teachers also need time to step back and observe what is going on, building up observations and notes about the students as individuals. No one knows the students' abilities to perform in class better than the teacher, and watching the students interact with their peers in the target language is the best indicator of their ability in the target language.

Let us call these *talking skills*; in other words, interactive communication using speaking and listening.

"How can we assess talking skills?"

Teachers traditionally asked students to read aloud, or do guided roleplays to assess speaking; and did lots of listening comprehensions – read by the teacher, or given on audio- or video-cassettes – to assess listening.

However, teachers would spend their time better in observing the students interact than in giving daily listening comprehensions. The result of the listening comprehension tells you very little. The only times students listen in this way is to announcements, the radio, or perhaps the phone. If the student doesn't understand, the teacher doesn't know why.

- Is it because of the level of linguistic complexity? (structures? vocabulary?)
- Is it because of the quality or audibility of the tape?
- Is it because of the complexity of the questions?
- Is it because of the inefficiency of the distractors (SEE PAGE 36) in the listening comprehension questions?

Assessing students through observation is something we do all the time. In fact, if exam results don't match our observed assessment, we often change or over-ride the exam result. What is difficult is to formalise this informal procedure, e.g. sometimes a student's fluency can impress us so much that we don't notice how many structural mistakes he/she is making.

PROFILING can help. We can choose one aspect of talking skills as today's criterion, and watch the class to measure their performance on this criterion alone. This will hopefully break down a general gut feeling about a student's performance into a number of PROFILE assessments.

Here are some possible areas where you could note individual students' contributions.

- How accurate is their use of structures? Their pronunciation? Their spelling?
- Do they use a wide range of structures? Vocabulary? Linkers?
- Can they vary their language so that it is socially appropriate (e.g. formal, friendly, etc.)?
- Can they interrupt, take turns, and generally carry on a natural conversation in the target language?
- Are their contributions the right length? On the right subject?
- How much of a strain is it to listen to them?

And, more arguably:

- Do they contribute frequently to the class or do they avoid participation?
- Do they have good ideas?

Which do we choose? We said above that a student's fluency can hide his/her structural mistakes. But this may be a good thing. We may want to encourage fluency, and not worry about structural accuracy. This is why it is vitally important to make sure that our assessment criteria are set via CONGRUENT EVALUATION (SEE PAGE 33) – in other words, why, what and how we assess should match the aims of our teaching programme.

As with writing, we can use marking schemes, PROFILES and BANDS. You can find these in books, but it is better if you use a standard set of PROFILES agreed between all the language teachers in your school. PROFILES could be the same for French, Spanish, Polish, etc. These should then be translated and sent to all the students (and their parents).

Using PROFILES and other schemes to break down talking skills into sub-skills means that you will have to assess students over time: we will return to this when discussing CONTINUOUS ASSESSMENT in Chapter 11.

Summary

We have seen here how assessment can be used to help students learn as well as test them. Both ANALYTIC MARKING SCHEMES and PROFILING are used to assess students especially for writing and speaking. PROFILING, however, gives students more information.

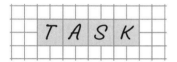

In this chapter, we listed some possible areas where you could note individual students' contributions.

Arrange a meeting with the other language teachers in your school – don't forget to include the teachers of the students' L1. If this is not possible, imagine you are in such a meeting. Take a copy/copies of PHOTOCOPIABLE PAGE 4.

What would you add to the list? What would you put in the gaps?

In your opinion, which of the sub-skills listed are the most important?

From your knowledge of the tests that the school uses, which do you think the school thinks are the most important?

How often in a school year would you want to focus on each sub-skill?

With the other teachers, make a photocopiable checklist (or add to this list) that you can use in class that concentrates on the areas which are of importance to your school's students, administration and parents. Can you also turn this list into a chart for recording students' contributions?

CHAPTER 10

Assessing procedures and attitudes

Traditionally, teachers have judged students, through tests, assessments, analysis of their work, and so on. However, as we have seen in this book, it is very difficult to measure a student's ability accurately. In the end, there is only one person who knows how much they are learning: the student.

Earlier in this book, we looked at INDIRECT versus DIRECT TESTING. ◆ SEE PAGE 30 Suppose we extend this concept to assessment. We have two choices: interpret data about the students to assess their abilities or involve them in their assessment.

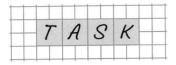

What are the advantages of involving students in their own assessment?

What problems can you foresee for these people?

the student
the teacher
teachers of other subjects
parents
the school's administration
the school's resources

Reason 1: The real question

There is really only one question that can assess a learner: *Do you feel you have improved?* If the learner (honestly) thinks he/she is better, and the teacher doesn't, who is right? If the learner (honestly) thinks he/she is no better, but the teacher disagrees, who is right?

In the Introduction, we emphasised that learning is an individual action – you can study in groups, but you can't learn in groups. Improvement, or lack of it, is therefore what the learner **feels**. Of course, they may not say what they really think as they may:

… be lying to get extra marks
… think that you want them to say they have improved
… not want to look stupid in front of their friends
… not want to look too clever in front of their friends.

Reason 2: It's your job to teach …

The traditional testing system puts no responsibility on the student. The student is accustomed to the teacher saying if he/she is good or bad. Many students approach tests hoping that, this time, they will be lucky. For many students assessment is something that teachers do **to** them, rather than something teachers do **with** them.

However, if we see evaluation as part of the teaching process, we can use assessment to help students learn their strengths and weaknesses and plan their learning better. We can encourage them to become self-critical and to take more responsibility. This may sound impossibly idealistic but, as we shall see, we already do this to some extent, and it can be done quite easily with a bit of planning (see below and especially true of APPRAISALS, PAGE 75).

Reason 3: Not all learning follows the teacher's plan

It is obvious that students don't always learn everything we teach. On the other hand, it must also be true that they learn things we don't teach, otherwise they would never be able to create a sentence they hadn't heard in class.

The teacher's job is traditionally to:

… predict where students may have problems with a language item or text

… plan how to help students to learn these problem areas

… assess students' ability in these areas and decide what to do next.

However, this leaves two areas.

- What about the problems they have that we haven't anticipated?

- What about the learning they do that we haven't anticipated?

Let us look at these in more detail.

Problems they have that we haven't anticipated

If the teacher suddenly finds the (majority of the) class has a problem in an unexpected area, he/she will normally do one of the following.

- Make a note and teach the item in the future.

- Do a quick exposition of the item in question. This might range from translating or miming an unknown word, to writing rules and substitution tables on the board.

- Tell the students to ignore the item because it's not important (e.g. an unknown word in a skimmed text).

These items will probably not be included in any formal test because it has been assumed that the students have already mastered them.

Learning they do that we haven't anticipated

On the other hand, if a student has a question about a text, this might mean that he/she may be ready to learn it. Let's call this the SALIENCY EFFECT.

We have all had the experience, when learning a foreign language, of suddenly noticing an unknown word, phrase or construction being used time and time again. It suddenly sticks out or becomes *salient*. This might be a word the teacher uses all the time (e.g. *Brilliant!* or *Your turn*); or a word or phrase from a song or TV advertisement. We ask someone what it means, and we continue to notice it for a couple of weeks. Then the word seems to disappear.

This would imply that there may be a time when, for us as individuals, that word is suddenly extra-noticeable. It seems obvious that this would be the ideal time to teach the individual the item and so respond to their insight. However, there are two problems.

- What is suddenly salient for one individual will probably not be salient for the whole class; if a beginner has suddenly started to hear the word *would* in conditional sentences (e.g. the teacher always says *Vincente, what would you say?*), and asks the teacher to explain it, the teacher may say that this is too advanced and that they'll learn it later.

- What the individual is ready to learn will probably not fit in with the teacher's plan. If the teacher is practising skimming, and a student asks what a particular word means, the teacher would probably tell them the word wasn't important because they are practising skim-reading.

Evaluation of these items

Obviously, none of these salient items will be included in any formal test, because they are unlikely to be on the syllabus. However, the individual student's ability to question and work out language problems for him/herself is a vital language-learning skill – perhaps the most important skill of all. If we are really interested in the student's learning processes and attitudes, these items – the student's personal learning syllabus – should be recorded and the student given credit.

How can we get this data from the student?

We will now look at various techniques for getting this kind of data from the student. Some of these ideas are based on what we already do. Others are a bit more unfamiliar.

TASK

Read the list of techniques in the table below. Tick the correct boxes.

	Already do it	Tried it already	Never heard of it
Confidence rating			
Checklists			
Learned lists			
Learner diaries			
Redesign and analyse a class			
Self-reports			
Student tests			
Clinics			

1 Confidence rating

One very simple and quick option open to the teacher is to include CONFIDENCE RATINGS in any test. By simply adding a column of numbers next to any test, you will be able to compare what the student thinks he/she can do with what the student can actually do, e.g.

Write a suitable form of the verb (one word only) in each space.
Contractions count as one word.
Then for each answer, tick one of the numbers 0-6.
Tick 6 if you are completely sure the answer is correct.
Tick 4 if you think the answer is probably correct.
Tick 2 if you are not confident about the answer.
Tick 0 if you have no idea or are guessing.

1) He _____ to the cinema every day.   (go)   6 4 2 0

2) On Tuesday he _____ to go to the cinema.   (like)   6 4 2 0

This will give you very useful information for future APPRAISALS. People will tend to fall into the following categories:

	Confident (6/4)	Unconfident (2/0)
Answer right	Self-aware	No self-belief
Answer wrong	Over-confident	Self-aware

Apart from giving you a PROFILE of the student, this is another example of assessment as teaching. Part of our job as teachers is to encourage students to become more aware of their abilities (or lack of them), and to help them work on those areas. Completing CONFIDENCE RATINGS helps them to develop this skill.

Note: Remember that students who are familiar with BANDS and PROFILES can also assess their essay before giving it to the teacher to assess. Every mistake in their essay is something they haven't been able to find themselves. On getting the teacher's assessment, they compare it with their own and teacher and student discuss any problems or issues arising.

TIP

This is a simple model that we can use more generally.

1 Give the students a task.

2 The students complete the task.

3 The students assess their own performance on the task.

4 The teacher assesses the students' performance on the task.

5 They meet and compare assessments.

6 The teacher can then change the teaching programme if necessary.

7 The students can change their learning programme (e.g. via useful items to include in their learning plan in their next APPRAISAL).

2 Checklists

By a 'checklist', we mean a version of the SYLLABUS suitable for students. This SYLLABUS:

… may possibly (but not necessarily) be a simplified version

… will use the teacher's linguistic terms (e.g. present simple for routine actions)

… will also give an example (e.g. *On Mondays he normally goes to the cinema*).

Remember that you will probably need to give students these concrete examples of the language items you want to teach, or of how you measure a sub-skill. Students do not share our teaching vocabulary: we have to teach them it.

Remember that by SYLLABUS, we do not necessarily limit ourselves to linguistic items. We could also include:

… language learning skills: *finding a word in a dictionary in 30 seconds*

… learning skills: *organising lesson notes so that student can find item in 30 seconds*

… behavioural items: *works in groups responsibly and without causing disruption*

… schooling skills: *misses two homeworks per term or fewer*.

"Why should students have checklists?"

● To plan their learning and to let the students know which parts of the SYLLABUS you think are the most important. We can't expect the student to remember every single thing we teach them. From our own experiences, we know that we forget things that we do not regularly use. So it is important that we tell the students that, e.g. we think the present simple is more important than types of transport. This allows them to prepare their own learning and their revision – a vital learning skill.

● To allow them to assess their own performance and progress.

"How do we do checklists?" At the start of the new school year, we can give the students a list of what they are expected to learn. The teacher may well need to go through the list with the students to make sure that they understand the items on the list.

Of course, the list could be in L1, although it is obviously better to write it in English if possible – remember it is good classroom-authentic language!

Next to this list you could add a grid of boxes for self- or negotiated assessment. Clearly state a set of marks and definitions at the top, e.g.

```
6 I am very sure about this item.

4 I will get this item right more often than I will
  get it wrong.

2 I will get this item wrong more often than I will
  get it right.

0 I have no idea what this item is.
```

TIP

Always try and give even numbers for this kind of exercise. If you ask the students to self-assess on odd numbers, they will normally choose the middle one.

```
5 Excellent

4 Very good

3 Good

2 Not very good

1 Terrible
```

Almost every student will compromise and go for 3.

Page 62 shows an example of a checklist that might be appropriate for elementary students.

Note how, at the start of any teaching programme, many of the items will be completely new to the students, but it is important to include them as it gives them something to tick off as they go through the year. The checklist then becomes a visible record of progress, and, hopefully, motivates the students who are impressed by their learning ability. SEE RECORD KEEPING (PAGE 70) for more details.

Example checklist

6 I am very sure about this item.

4 I will get this item right more often than I will get it wrong.

2 I will get this item wrong more often than I will get it right.

0 I have no idea what this item is.

Verb forms: **Confidence rating:**

Present simple: *to be* +	*My name is Juan.*	....
Present simple: *to be* ?	*Are you English?*	....
Present simple: *to be* –	*He isn't a doctor.*	....
Present simple: routines +	*On Tuesdays, he goes to the cinema.*	....
Present simple: routines ?	*Do you come here a lot?*	....
Present simple: routines –	*I don't like going to discos.*	....

Vocabulary fields: open

jobs	*doctor, police officer,* etc.	....
food and drink	*cheese, coffee,* etc.	....
shops and places	*cinema, home, supermarket,* etc.	....

Vocabulary fields: closed

adverbs of frequency	*How often?, always, often,* etc.	
pronouns: subject/object/ poss.	*I, me, my, her,* etc.	....

Pronunciation:

/æ/ vs /ʌ/	*cat* vs *cut*	....
/ɪ/ vs /iː/	*chip* vs *cheap*	....
/k/ vs /t/ vs /p/	*piCK* vs *hiT* vs *liP*	....

Learning skills:

organising notes to find answer in 30 seconds	....
learning and using the classroom language on the poster in the classroom	....
contributing to group- and classwork	....
finding a word in a bilingual dictionary in less than 30 seconds	....
doing all the homework	....

3 Learned lists

Checklists tell the teacher what the students think they have learned. They also tell the teacher what the students think they are good or bad at. We can investigate this area of assessment further through using a 'learned list' – we simply ask the students what they (think they) have learned.

But remember that the students will probably need prompts, as students and teachers often have different ways of describing the same thing. You may want to give students concrete examples of the language items (forms and meanings?) you want to teach, or concrete examples of how you measure a sub-skill.

Asking them to write down what they have learned can then be used in different ways, e.g. as part of:

... a CONTINUOUS ASSESSMENT procedure (PAGE 69)
... the checklist revision procedure (PAGE 72)
... a learner diary (below)
... a portfolio (PAGE 73).

4 Learner diaries

Every lesson, or week, the students make an entry in a diary describing their learning that lesson/week.

The diary can simply be pages added to the back of a file, or it could be a template designed by the teacher. The weekly/monthly entry may cover:

... lists and examples of what the student has covered (e.g. vocabulary
   items/structures)
... tips, ideas and checklists of what the student has covered (e.g. paragraphing)
... notes, insights, cultural tips, set phrases
... comments about the class.

Note that the diary should ideally cover what the students feel they have learned, rather than what the teacher thinks they have done in class. This is a difficult skill for a student to learn, and it may require awareness raising by the teacher to make the students write about what they think and feel.

If we agree that students don't learn everything we teach them in class, by occasionally reading (extracts from) their diaries, teachers can assess the mismatch between their teaching and their students' learning. The extracts will also tell us what they have learned that has not been (overtly) taught. By comparing what the student has learned with what we have taught, we can gain a lot of useful information for the FORMATIVE EVALUATION (SEE PAGE 32) of the teaching programme.

By definition, diaries are normally personal and private. You should therefore set clear guidelines about how much access you will have to the diaries.

The diaries could either be collected and read, say, twice a term. Read two or three each weekend, or you will have one weekend to read thirty diaries! Alternatively, you can tell the class that you will not read the diaries but will ask the students for extracts or copies of pages they would like to show you. These pages, or the whole diary if not private, can constitute part of a portfolio (SEE PAGE 73). Have a look at the example of a sample page for a learner diary on PHOTOCOPIABLE PAGE 5. Use this as a model for use in your class/school.

Note: By asking students what their problems were from previous classes, you can build up an 'agenda' of things to discuss in future classes or clinics (SEE PAGE 67).

5 Re-design/analyse a lesson (via learned lists)

One way you can evaluate students' progress and the effect you are having upon it is to share the lesson-planning process with the students. Initially, this might seem a bit threatening. But if it is true that learners learn things we don't consciously teach, and don't learn things that we do actually teach, it might be worth asking them what they have learned and how they (think they) have learned it.

Once again, students are not normally asked these questions, so they will find it difficult to give you an answer – they won't know the vocabulary of teaching, lesson-planning, and so on.

However, in the last few minutes of a lesson, you can:

… ask them what they think they have learned

… ask them to re-design the lesson so that it would be more helpful next time you teach it.

Hand the students a (simplified) version of your lesson plan, e.g.

> My lesson plan was:
>
> 1 WARMER: alphabet on board; think of a sport for each letter
>
> 2 MINGLE: produce a class graph/bar chart of the class's favourite sport(s)
>
> 3 PRESENTATION: sts read the rules of rugby in groups
>
> 4   elicit words about football
>
> 5 PRACTICE: sts in groups rewrite paragraph so that it gives the rules of football
>
> 6 EXTENSION: sts in groups write the rules of (another of) their favourite sports
>
> 7 LEARNING AWARENESS: sts in groups write rules of English lessons in school
>
> 8   sts write penalties if these rules are broken

You could then ask questions similar to the following.

- Rank the parts of the lesson in the order you enjoyed them.
- Which bits were the most useful?
- Where did you speak most/least?
- Did you prefer moving around, working in groups or working by yourself?
- Did you all speak the same amount or did some speak more than others?
- If you had the lesson again, how would you change it? Why?
- Would you have liked that class if it had been done in your L1?
- Would you have learned anything/more/less if it had been done in your L1?

This will make the students think about the language learning and teaching process. Once again, it is an awareness-raising process, asking the students to think about what they do in class and how the process could be made more useful and/or effective. How the students respond should give you a strong idea about how they approach a lesson, and how they think they learn.

6 Self-reports

As teachers we often take responsibility away from the students when it comes to assessment. They can then put all the onus of evaluation on to us, and so they can blame the teacher for their lack of progress rather than blaming the person most directly responsible – themselves. What we need, then, is a way of encouraging students to take on their own evaluation.

If we let them play teacher, we can go one stage further and ask them to write their own reports. This may cause the usual problems of:

Trust: Will they abuse this opportunity and simply write themselves good reports?

… often they are harder on themselves or others than the teacher.

… results must be negotiated and agreed.

Reliability: How can we moderate their reports?

… set up moderation groups as we do for teachers.

… results must be negotiated and agreed using the same criteria as we do.

Threat: The teacher feels nervous about giving the students so much power.

… remember the students are equally unused to power and equally nervous.

… it is time the student took responsibility for bad work, rather than the teacher.

… every mistake the student can't or won't find, the teacher has to. It saves time!

What might a student report look like? As similar as possible to the school's existing one.

Look at the report your school currently uses.

What kind of information is required?

Are there any parts that students could not complete for themselves? Why?

Are there any parts that students could not be taught to complete for themselves? Why?

7 Student-written tests

Like student reports, many teachers might be worried about asking their students to write their own tests. How useful would the results be? Won't they cheat? Won't they just ask easy questions?

It is easy to understand why teachers might ask these questions, but this is because they are thinking of the results of the test, rather than the evaluation (and learning) opportunities this process offers.

Imagine that Group A writes ten questions for Group B. In traditional testing, you would record the results of Group B. For evaluation purposes, you would look at the work of Group A. Students don't know very much about testing theory. They will therefore all tend to write questions which are either not reliable or not valid, e.g. one question might be:

1 He _____ to the cinema.

The teacher can then explain that the answer could be *goes/went/will go/has been/will have gone/would like to go/is addicted,* etc. The students are then in a position where they must demonstrate their understanding of the meaning of the structure in order to limit the other students' answers. For example, if they are trying to test the present simple, they must show routine: ... *on Tuesdays* ... and also choose a living person (the teacher?) to make sure that the other students don't use the past simple. This still allows for various answers, so they may need to include the verb (*go*), and possibly limit the number of words that the other students can write in the space (*one word only, contractions count as one word*). This also helps them learn and better understand instructions in the target language (e.g. *suitable*). This gives us:

> Write a suitable form of the verb in the gap (one word only; contractions count as one word).
>
> **1)** On Tuesdays, Luisa normally _____ to the cinema.   (go)

This still leaves several possible problems: they could still write *went*. But then they and the other group will have to argue about exactly what we want them to discuss: the possible meanings of this structure. This is an extremely powerful learning device as it:

... forces them to think about meaning as well as structure
... teaches them useful test vocabulary (*gap, suitable form of verb*, etc.)
... teaches them useful test conventions, such as 'contractions count as one word'
... shows them the importance of reading the test rubric/instructions
... teaches them to look for the answer the teacher/tester wants.

While they are discussing the questions, the teacher has an opportunity to assess their level of knowledge, their contributions to the group, and so on. All this information is extremely useful: in a test, you see what the student thinks the answer is, but not why the student thinks that is the answer. The students may conduct their discussion in L1 – this is valid as the result is in English. Here you see not only the result, but also the process.

Useful information gathered from listening to these groups at work should be recorded – word for word, if possible – and used as a concrete example when doing APPRAISALS. ◆ SEE PAGE 75

The teacher can also collect the tests and copy them, and ask the students who wrote them to put them in their portfolio. ◆ SEE PAGE 73

Variation

Give the students the subject of the test.

Each student can write one question on a slip of paper, e.g.

| Student A: | Mr Brown normally _____ to the cinema on Tuesdays. |
| | a) go   b) goes   c) gone   d) been |

| Student B: | *She likes sunbathing. [make negative]* |

| Student C: | My father / drive / a red Mercedes |

| Student D: | She _____ in Zaragoza. (live) |

- The teacher collects these and then photocopies the questions (or writes them on another piece of paper) and distributes them to the class.
- The students then answer all the questions.
- They pass the paper to the next student, who marks the question he/she wrote.
- They pass the papers again, and mark their question again.
- They continue to do this until every paper has been fully marked (i.e. with 30 students, they pass the paper on 30 times).
- The final student totals the marks: power!

TIP

We said above that students are not very good at writing tests because they don't know much about it (or is it because we want to keep these skills to ourselves?!).

One additional step after the test could be to rank the questions they wrote:

… which was the best? Why?
… which was the most difficult? Why?
… which was the most confusing? Why?
… would you change any of the questions for another class? How? Why?

Apart from helping you to assess their thought processes and language learning skills, this will help them to develop useful learning skills like understanding what the examiner wants.

Keep copies of the best questions: you can save time next year by using these in any tests you have to write!

Note: Students can, of course, mark each other's written work via PROFILES, BANDS, etc. (SEE PAGE 49) as well as testing grammar and/or vocabulary.

8 Clinics

The idea of a clinic is to hand over a small part of the SYLLABUS to the students. A section of a lesson (e.g. the last 20 minutes of the last class of each month) is dedicated to questions that the students raise. Remember, as we said above when discussing the SALIENCY EFFECT (SEE PAGE 58), when they ask the question is the time to teach it.

Most of these questions will be totally unrelated to each other and the SYLLABUS. They can range from grammar to information to questions about the SYLLABUS. They can sometimes be quite complicated, too.

Ask if they have any questions and/or comments about language, language learning, or the teaching programme and write these on the board like the agenda for a meeting. Then jointly decide which are the most interesting and go through them, explaining or asking for explanations as necessary.

If there are questions you cannot answer immediately, you should say they are too complicated for an instant answer, and write them on the agenda for the next clinic session. Start each clinic with answers to outstanding questions from the last one.

The power of clinics: a story

In one clinic, my students asked me how to use *just*. Being a boringly typical teacher, I immediately started my stock lesson on *just* and the present perfect, as in *I've just seen him*. I had just finished, when they said *No. no. The **other** meanings of 'just'*. I had no idea – no one had ever asked me this before. I put it on the agenda for the next clinic: I needed a week or two to work out how to explain or ignore the other 14 uses!

Clinics are always interesting as students ask some unusual and insightful questions. Of course, each individual is interested in different things, so clinic-teaching cannot be included in a formal test. However, we can make notes about good ideas and/or interesting explanations and use these as part of any one individual's assessment.

Summary

In this chapter, we looked at why we should involve our students in assessment.

Reason 1: Do you feel you have improved? How can we find out if how they see their progress matches how we see their progress?

Reason 2: It's your job to teach ... Traditional testing puts no responsibility on the student – assessment is something that teachers do **to** them, rather than something teachers do **with** them.

Reason 3: Not all learning follows the teacher's plan. Students both have problems and also do learning that we haven't anticipated.

We have also looked at involving the student in the **procedures** of evaluation by using:

1 Confidence ratings
2 Checklists
3 Learned lists
4 Learner diaries
5 Redesign and analyse a class
6 Self-reports
7 Student tests
8 Clinics

All of these techniques attempt to look at student data in a non-traditional way: they are concerned with developing the students' awareness of their own abilities and how they learn best. They all involve delegating power and responsibility to the student. The teacher cannot evaluate the student's learning attitudes and procedures without releasing some power. This is because we can only evaluate these attitudes and procedures by asking and involving the student.

This may all be new behaviour – for both teacher and student – and we need to be prepared for the occasional disaster! However, none of these ideas are totally new to any teacher – we all do them already to some extent, e.g.

● 1 Confidence ratings

In class, we already say to students *Are you sure?*

● 2 Checklists

We already recycle SYLLABUS items in later lessons to remind students of what they've learned.

● 3 Learned lists

We already start classes by saying *What did we do last lesson?*

Look down the list above again, and try and think of things you already do that involve the same skills and concepts. Now look at each technique and try to think of ways you can build on your existing practice – what the students are already familiar with. How can you delegate more responsibility to the student?

PART D Assessing over time

CHAPTER 11

Continuous assessment

"What is continuous assessment?"

It is no different from any other form of assessment – it simply refers to how frequently you test or evaluate the students. The results of these 'samples' are collected over a period of time and the student is assessed on not just one performance, but many performances. This raises the following issues.

- How often should we sample the students?
- Which 'performances' should we sample?
- How do we put all the different results together into a single assessment?

Answer the three questions above for your school's current system.

Answer the three questions for your experience as a) a schoolchild; and b) a university student.

Has there been any change?

"How often should we sample the students?"

As teachers, we already assess the students on every single thing they do or say: we are constantly building up a picture or a PROFILE of that student in our minds; we could 'place' them without giving them a formal test. The simple difference with a formal system of CONTINUOUS ASSESSMENT is that we keep formal written records of the students' ability to perform.

How often we make notes about their performance will largely depend on the size of the class. It is more difficult to form a mental picture of six classes of 40 students than to make extensive notes about a single class of fifteen students.

A formal system of CONTINUOUS ASSESSMENT may make a difference in the amount we test. If we are assessing over, say, a year, it will be better to do lots of small assessments rather than lots of assessments the size of a formal end-of-year test.

"Which 'performances' should we sample?"

Throughout this book we have listed the different skills required to be a successful language learner and user. Which skills you need to formally assess will only partly be your choice: the state, your school, and your Head of Department will require certain assessment information, as will the student's parents. You may well want to add other criteria to help you arrive at a personal decision concerning each student, such as participation in group work, or using the target language when the teacher isn't looking. Such items may not be formally required, but may reflect a student attitude that leads to better performance.

"How do we put all the different results together into a single assessment?"

Once again, the state, your school, and your Head of Department may require you to compile assessment information in a standardised way. However, like all forms of assessment, the final balance between a strong performance in one area and a weak performance in another will largely depend on the teacher's judgement.

In general, give priority to:

… language use (talking and writing skills) rather than language components (tests on individual structural items, vocabulary, etc.)

… results of direct testing (e.g. writing letters) rather than indirect testing (e.g. editing texts)

… elements that are seen as valuable in the student's final assessment process (i.e. the weighting will probably depend upon BACKWASH from the state's assessment process)

… the student's learning strategies, e.g. the ability to use resources, make him/herself understood, make analogies, etc.

However you collate the information, the most important thing is to keep the records that allow you to make the final decision. This brings us on to record-keeping.

Record-keeping

Every teacher benefits from good record-keeping. These benefits are most obvious when the student moves to another teacher, either in a year or when moving from year to year.

This is also where the enormous difference between NORM-REFERENCED and CRITERIA-REFERENCED testing appears. NORM-REFERENCED results may be useful to employers and even the state, who are dealing with vast numbers of people and need a kind of selective shorthand. But knowing whether a student is in the top or bottom quarter of the class does not help the teacher to help the student.

Let us look at how we treat these various forms of assessment over time. This section will look at assessing the student vis-a-vis the SYLLABUS – our teaching targets. We can do this through:

… tests over time

… mini-tests and checktests over time.

We can also use checklists for the same purpose. ◆ SEE CHAPTER 12

1 Tests over time

We have seen in the first part of this book how difficult it is to write a valid and reliable formal test. However, tests are still probably the most common form of assessment. Even if they are neither valid nor reliable, they still have great FACE VALIDITY. ◆ SEE PAGE 20 Many schools, teachers, students and parents actually like tests. Why is this?

Imagine that at the moment your school assesses its students only on an end-of-year test which comprises:

… a gap-fill test of vocabulary

… multiple-choice grammar test

… ten multiple-choice questions for both listening and reading comprehension

… a writing test of a personal letter describing yourself to a penfriend.

Would you change your test? How would you change it? Look at the roles on PAGE 71 and, for each role, decide a) whether you would change it and b) how you would change it.

Roles for task

Minister of Education

A clever student who is good at all subjects but is hopeless at languages and may have to repeat the year because of his poor marks in language tests

A teacher who is going to retire next year

A school Head who has just been promoted and wants to 'shake up' the school

A native-speaker parent of the target language whose child got only 60% in the last test.

It seems difficult to imagine that we can avoid giving tests, even though we know that there are severe limitations on how accurate their results may be. The important thing, then, is to:

… make the test as good as possible

… try to make the test as helpful to the teaching process as possible

… use the results in an intelligent way.

2 Mini-tests and checktests over time

Many schools still use a large end-of-year test as a 'final decider'. Why is this? Perhaps it is because teachers like to have their opinions confirmed by some other objective decision-making tool.

But this might be unfair because a final test does not help the student learn. It is better to give tests early and often. This gives students the information they need: how hard they have to work and which areas they have to work on. It also gives them chance to improve.

So instead of giving one large end-of-year test, it is better to divide it into a number of smaller mini-tests. For example, instead of setting the students the task of answering 100 questions in an hour, we can set them 20 questions given in the last ten minutes over five classes throughout the term.

"Why should we do this?"

- It gives each student the chance to see their progress and build up their skills.
- It encourages the student to review his/her work from time to time. The first things we forget are things we don't use – occasional inclusion in a test will keep them simmering in the student's head.
- Give each test a different focus, so that you can build up a kind of componential list of the student's abilities.
- It gives weaker students something to aim for and gives them lots of fresh starts. ◆ SEE PAGE 24
- It helps students set themselves more realistic goals.
- It creates more dialogue between teacher and student about what they are doing.

You can base the mini-test items on items in the student's checklist – we could call this a checktest. You should keep a record of these tests as part of the CONTINUOUS ASSESSMENT process. Results should also be given to the student to keep in their portfolio. ◆ SEE PAGE 73

Summary

This chapter has dealt with CONTINUOUS ASSESSMENT and looked at frequency of testing, what we should test and how to record all the results.

CHAPTER 12

Formative evaluation

So far, we have looked at ways of recording the student's performance to use items on the SYLLABUS, through:

… tests over time

… mini-tests and checktests over time.

But remember that we are also interested in the student's attitudes to language and learning. We have seen in this book how we can ask students real questions: about what has worked for them, and about how much they feel they have learned. In other words, we have attempted to involve the student in the teaching and assessment procedure.

This involvement cannot only be done once or twice a year. If it is to benefit the student and the teaching programme, we must build this co-operation and responsibility into the foundations of the assessment procedure continuously over the year. This is what is meant by FORMATIVE EVALUATION: continuous mutual feedback.

This kind of information must also be recorded. Apart from learner diaries, we can also use PROFILES and checklists in a continuous way, as well as student portfolios.

1 Profiles over time

One of the advantages of PROFILES (SEE PAGE 49) is that they can build up a picture over time. For example, over a term, the student's writing profile (based on 0–5) might be as follows:

Task:	1	2	3	4	5
Relevance	2	2	3	3	4
Adequacy	2	2	3	2	3
Grammar	2	2	2	3	2
Vocabulary	2	2	. 2	2	2
Punctuation	2	3	3	3	2
'Profile'	10	11	13	13	13

This tells both the teacher and the student that – in general – he/she is learning how to organise essays better (relevance and adequacy – mostly non-linguistic skills). The marks for vocabulary and grammar vary more, but how much progress can we realistically expect over a term? Remember that a native speaker would get '5', so '3' is very good.

We could record the results of our observation of their writing and talking skills on PHOTOCOPIABLE PAGE 6.

2 Checklists over time

As we saw when discussing checklists (SEE PAGE 60), the students are asked to assess their confidence in different areas of the syllabus.

On the checklist, you should also include different times for assessment. By making the students look at their checklists again, we keep them thinking about the content of the course. But checklists not only encourage self-assessment, they also build confidence and guide students.

The first time we ask for self-assessment, the students will probably write '0'. The second time, there will be a mixture of '2's and '0's. At the end of the year, there should be mainly '4's and '6's. This lets the students see some element of progress over the year, which hopefully motivates them more.

On the other hand, checklists can also help with problems of over-confidence, or when students realise that in fact they don't understand something as well as they thought they did. For example, *will* and *going to* appear on the checklist. One or two students have a theory that *going to* is used for the 'near future' and *will* is used for the 'far future' so they mark the items as '6' because they think they are completely confident. They then learn in class that their explanation is wrong, so later in the year they change their '6' to a '4'.

Example checklist over time (based on page 62).

---

6 I am very sure about this item.
4 I will get this item right more often than I will get it wrong.
2 I will get this item wrong more often than I will get it right.
0 I have no idea what this item is.

Confidence rating:

Verb forms:		Time:	1	2	3	4	5	6
Present simple: *to be* +	*My name is Juan*		.....	.....	.....	.....	.....	.....
Present simple: *to be* ?	*Are you English?*		.....	.....	.....	.....	.....	.....
Present simple: *to be* –	*He isn't a doctor.*		.....	.....	.....	.....	.....	.....
Pres. simp. routines +	*On Tuesdays, he goes to the cinema.*		.....	.....	.....	.....	.....	.....
Pres. simp. routines ?	*Do you come here a lot?*		.....	.....	.....	.....	.....	.....
Pres. simp. routines –	*I don't like going to discos.*		.....	.....	.....	.....	.....	.....

---

3 Student portfolios

Artists keep all their best pieces of work in a portfolio so that they can show other people the range of what they can do.

Portfolios can also be used by students to keep pieces of work which they think best represents them. Of course, most of this will be written work (homework, essays, test scores, project work, etc.), although video- and audio-cassettes could also be included.

In this way, the portfolio concept is more powerful than a simple test result, because it shows not only what the student has done, but also gives the teacher an insight into the student's mind: he/she is proud of this piece of work, but not that one. In this way, the teacher can see what the student's sets of values are: where the student thinks he/she has made progress, and what he/she sees the strengths and weaknesses as being. It is, in a way, a variant of test CONFIDENCE RATING. ◆ SEE PAGE 59

Portfolios are also an excellent link between the school and the parent, allowing parents to see samples of the children's best work, while also being a showcase for the school's teaching. The parent can also become involved in helping the child decide what goes in – thus becoming a negotiating partner in the school's assessment process.

Guide to setting up a portfolio

It is important that a portfolio is built slowly: you don't want to have to go back through old pieces of work hunting out the good stuff. Explain to the students that when they think they have done a good piece of work, they should put it in the portfolio. You should also explain that they may want to review the contents from time to time. After all, what the student takes out of the portfolio is possibly more important to the teacher than what he/she puts in. We can assume that items removed means that the student feels he/she has covered that point or moved past that stage of language learning – the SALIENCY EFFECT is over. ➤ SEE PAGE 58

Privacy

As with learner diaries, you should agree how private the portfolio should be. When you come to formal evaluations with the student, you may want to ask the student to select items from the portfolio, rather than show you the whole thing. This selection is, in itself, a vital stage as it requires the learner to demonstrate some form of self-assessment and self-awareness.

Portfolios: possible contents

… test/mini-test results
… marked homework from language lessons or other subjects done in English
… project work (may have been written as part of a group)
… audio-cassettes
… video-cassettes
… interesting articles/texts/song lyrics, etc. the student has found/read/understood
… compositions
… pages/extracts from a learner diary
… checklists/learned lists
… previous reports/evaluations by teachers, peers, or self, e.g. BANDINGS/PROFILES
… lesson-redesigns; lesson analyses
… results of previous PERFORMANCE REVIEWS, previous school years, previous schools, etc.

Summary

In this chapter we have looked at ways to use FORMATIVE ASSESSMENT, this is continuous mutual feedback. We investigated the use of:

- profiles over time
- checklists over time
- student profiles.

Think of a student who you have taught for a long time and whom you know very well. Think of the work the student has done recently and decide which items you would include in the portfolio if you were that student.

What would there be most of in the portfolio? Why?

What would be missing? Why?

If possible, introduce the idea of portfolios to your students. Compare your ideas with what the student puts in the portfolio.

CHAPTER 13

Summative assessment: Appraisals and performance reviews

Appraisals

More and more organisations are using APPRAISALS to evaluate a person's performance, whether the person is a teacher, a police officer or a factory worker.

The APPRAISAL is normally an interview or a series of interviews with a superior, and covers the employee's past, present and future – their work, their problems, their attitudes, and their plans and ambitions. The result is normally a document – often called a PERFORMANCE REVIEW – containing both a review of the past and a plan for the future. This is a negotiated document – it is agreed and signed by both sides.

This document is then used as a basis for the next interview: Which of the plans were fulfilled? Which plans weren't? Why? Why not? The two sides agree how to update the review and the plans, and then sign the document again.

So we can see that a PERFORMANCE REVIEW is like a photograph of a person at one particular time. If we want to see how the employee – or appraisee – has developed, we can look at the series of reviews.

Let us imagine that a teacher is about to have a PERFORMANCE REVIEW with the head teacher: what evidence would they like to have to show the appraiser? A teacher doesn't want to be judged on the observation reports of, say, just two of their lessons. Teachers want the school to think about their contribution in the staff room, their work on various school projects, their level of knowledge of their subject, and so on.

Cover the list below.

Imagine that today is the day of your APPRAISAL interview with the Head of your school. He/She has asked you to bring any information or documents you think are useful, or show the work you have done over the year. What would you take? Compare your ideas with the list below.

- Observation reports
- Materials written
- Best lesson plans
- List of interesting/successful things you have achieved in that year
- List of meetings/seminars/conferences/training courses attended
- Results of your students' work
- Examples of your students' work

- Reading list of books you have read over the academic year
- Quotes from colleagues about your work
- Notes/letters from superiors or parents/students praising your work during the year
- Ideas for next year's work
- (Anticipated) Criticisms of the past year's work and explanations

If APPRAISALS are suitable for teachers, they are equally suitable for students. And we should assess students using the same range of evidence – is it representative to judge a student on the result of two tests?

Performance reviews: Why, who, when, and what?

Why do performance reviews?

A traditional testing system puts no responsibility on the students – they are accustomed to the teacher telling them if they are 'good' or 'bad'. Many students approach tests hoping that, this time, they will be 'lucky'. For many students, then, explaining their progress, providing evidence and having to convince the teacher of their skills, even planning the areas they want or need to work on – these will all be new concepts.

However, these concepts will make them think about what they have done, what they have learned and, perhaps, how they approached the learning task. It also, of course, produces an agreed plan for future action – again making the student aware of his/her responsibility in the process.

From this it is obvious that PERFORMANCE REVIEWS are not just an assessment process, but also an educative process.

Who does performance reviews?

Traditionally, teachers did reviews of performance. But as we have seen in this book, one of the purposes of this kind of evaluation is that it encourages students to be aware of their own progress: their attitudes and the way they learn. As students become increasingly skilled and confident in assessing performance, we can ask them to assess themselves or each other. For example, students can easily read and BAND/PROFILE each other's essays. ◆ SEE PAGE 49

Remember, however, that when they begin, they may need moderation to make sure they are all giving the same grade. Surprisingly, students normally under-estimate their abilities. For this reason, it is often better to let students start by assessing non-linguistic criteria (e.g. organisation, handwriting, interest, etc.), where their opinion carries the same weight as the teacher's.

Eventually, of course, students could be assessed on their ability to assess their own work accurately. As we have seen, some exams already test what they call editing skills – finding grammatical mistakes or missing/redundant vocabulary in various texts written by other students. There is no reason why this couldn't be extended to assessing 'adequacy of content', 'completion of task' and other semi-linguistic skills.

Example

At the end of term, I asked a class to assess (via BANDS) their own talking and writing skills. They then came and discussed the band they had chosen with me. Most had underestimated themselves by one BAND. One student, though, had given himself a very high band for speaking. We talked about it, but still disagreed. I asked him to go and talk to another student, and get a second opinion from him. He asked me *What shall I talk about?* I suggested that he explained the problem to the student, and then he should ask the student to band him. Five minutes later, the second student came up to me, sadly shaking his head. He agreed with me. The first student looked unhappy, but what could he say? He had been judged by his peers.

The biggest problem for us as teachers is learning to change the way we see assessment. Teachers are accustomed to telling students what their 'results' are. It will feel difficult – and professionally threatening – suddenly to have to negotiate with an individual student. And students too may well be surprised at 'Teacher' consulting or counselling them about their performance as a partner-in-learning rather than figure of authority. Students may prefer to avoid responsibility.

This is a new process: we will all – teacher, student and educational institution – have to go very slowly. We may expect to make mistakes, but we will learn from these and learn new skills.

When to do performance reviews

PERFORMANCE REVIEWS may be part of either the FORMATIVE or SUMMATIVE EVALUATION process (SEE PAGE 32). The main difference between these will be what to do with the result. The review normally looks at continuing performance. However, teachers can add a summative element by finishing the review with the negotiation of a final grade.

What to cover in a performance review

Appraisal evidence

An APPRAISAL interview is a negotiated process: at the end you want an agreed document. However, you and the student may have very different ideas about his/her performance. Areas that you think are important may not seem important to him/her, and vice versa.

So it is important that both the teacher and the student take concrete examples of what they want to talk about to the interview.

What documents are available for you to use as evidence? Cover the section below and make a list. Then compare your list with the list below.

Possibly some or all of the following documents are available

Results:

… of various assessments that you have made, such as 'formal tests' or mini tests

… from bits of homework, or written or oral classwork marked using BANDS and PROFILES

… of the student's previous PERFORMANCE REVIEWS – especially plans that the student made in the past. (**Note:** you may have to get this from another teacher – possibly the teacher who taught them last year.)

Copies of:

... 'official' documents, such as BANDS, PROFILES and checklists you use.
... the student's work itself to illustrate your points better.

Notes:

... that you made about the student that arose during clinics
... from when students were analysing or redesigning lessons
... about the student in general.

The learner's evidence:

We will also need various records from the learner. So what would we like the student to bring to an APPRAISAL interview?

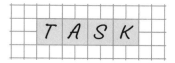

What information would we like the students to bring – apart from test results – that would help us assess the student's performance? Write a list of useful sources of information available.

Compare your list with the list we gave when talking about student portfolios on PAGE 73. Now compare your list with the list you gave when talking about the teacher's evidence on PAGE 77.

Stages in an appraisal: An example

"When should I do the appraisal?"

This will depend on the purpose of the APPRAISAL. You will almost certainly need to do one at the end of each academic year: a SUMMATIVE EVALUATION of the year's work. However, it is obviously impossible with large classes to have ten or 15 minutes with each student in the last couple of lessons in each year.

For this reason, it is best to have a system of 'rolling appraisals', in other words, in some lessons you do one or two students while the rest of the class does other work. If you follow this system all through the year, you can use the last two or three classes to have a quick word with the students who have the oldest PERFORMANCE REVIEW. Ask them if they want to add anything to their records or tell them of any new information you want to include.

Example

In the example below, a teacher has a class of 30 students (St1 – St30). Each week, they have three lessons of one hour each. There are two terms of 15 weeks each.

At the start of the third week, the teacher starts a system of interviewing two students per class while the rest of the class do project work. They mainly talk about what they have done before this course, how good the student thinks he/she is at (English), what his/her interests are, and other 'getting to know you' – as learner and person – areas. After they have all been interviewed, the teacher has a clinic (SEE PAGE 67) where common problems and questions are dealt with, and a summary of what they will concentrate on during the year is given.

From Week 10, the teacher has a second round of shorter interviews with each student, amending plans now that the information from the whole class is available. At the end of term, the teacher has a short question-and-answer session, followed by a mini-achievement test.

In Week 8 of the second term, the teacher gives the class the yearly ACHIEVEMENT TEST. After marking the test, the teacher has another round of interviews with the students to give them feedback and look at individual problem areas. The teacher re-teaches the most common problems and gives a mini-test on these at the end of term. The students who are much stronger or weaker than the rest of the class are then interviewed.

Week	Term 1 Lesson 1	Lesson 2	Lesson 3	Term 2 Lesson 1	Lesson 2	Lesson 3
1						
2						
3	St1/St2	St3/4	St5/6			
4	St7/8	St9/10	St11/12			
5	St13/14	St15/16	St17/18			
6	St19/20	St21/22	St23/24			
7	St25/26	St27/28	St29/30			
8		Clinic 1	Clinic 2	Yearly Achievement Test		
9				St1/St2	St3/4	St5/6
10	St1/St2	St3/4	St5/6	St7/8	St9/10	St11/12
11	St7/8	St9/10	St11/12	St13/14	St15/16	St17/18
12	St13/14	St15/16	St17/18	St19/20	St21/22	St23/24
13	St19/20	St21/22	St23/24	St25/26	St27/28	St29/30
14	St25/26	St27/28	St29/30	Mini-test	Results/feedback	
15	Clinic	Test		Mini-appraisals with 'difficult cases'		

- Ideally, it is best to give the 'big test' early so that students have a chance to look at their performance and modify it. You can then identify the most common problems the students have and re-teach them. You can then include these in a mini-test at the end of term to check learning. Is this 'cheating'? I don't think so. Our job is surely to help the students to learn, rather than to try and trip them up through tricky tests!

- It is important to have an early interview with each student to set goals and establish possible problems early in the year. This is fairer as it gives the student plenty of warning as to where their strengths and, more importantly in this case, their weaknesses are. These can be put in their learning plan.

- You can devote the last few lessons to interviews with 'problem' students, i.e. those who are much weaker, much stronger, or those with behavioural or other problems that need to be established in their final APPRAISAL.

- By putting the 'big test' before the final APPRAISALS, this sends a clear message to the student that their performance in the test only represents a part of their total assessment. This is a good example of methodological beneficial BACKWASH (SEE PAGE 28). If you have final APPRAISALS before the 'big test' students will assume that the test is more important than the interview.

- It is important to use the information gathered in the interviews in a kind a summarising clinic where you tell the class the major points which have come up. If you don't do this, they may see the interviews as having no point and the beneficial BACKWASH may be lost. For more information on clinics SEE PAGE 67.

Look at the schedule of interviews given on page 79.

Think about the structure of your school year and the size of a typical class you have to teach. Would the schedule look very different in your case?

Write a plan for next year.

"What happens in the appraisal interview?"

As the majority of the interviews will have to be quite short, it is very important that both sides are fully prepared. Teachers should provide the students with the following.

… the dates of the appraisal meeting
… a brief agenda
… a copy of the student's previous plan
… a blank outline for the next plan
… any scores from the (term's) work that are relevant
… attendance records
… copies of any criteria used to measure the student's work.

It may be useful to ask the students to sign these and suggest their own agenda items. This sounds complex, but doesn't need to be, e.g.

Example Agenda

To: Miguel
Appraisal Interview date: 4th May

I would like to talk about:
1 your handwriting
2 your 'postcard' homework
3 your mini-test result on pres. simple

You would like to talk about:
1 _____
2 _____
3 _____

Your last plan said you would look at:
1 your handwriting
2 your present simple question forms
3 talking English in class instead of Spanish

Ideas for your next plan:
1 _____
2 _____
3 _____

Your results so far this term

Checktests	Marks
March Mini-test	13/20
April Mini-test	12/20

Your homework average is   10/20

Attendance this year: 57   classes out of   60

Please fill in the gaps and return this to me.

Remember to bring any work you want to show me, as well as your copy of the speaking and writing profiles in case we need to look at them.

Thank you.

There is a blank APPRAISAL agenda on PHOTOCOPIABLE PAGE 7.

Appraisal day

"What should the teacher do on the day?"

Prepare three key topics

The interview is not very long, so time is limited. It is probably unrealistic to think that you can cover more than three major points in the interview, even if the student has hundreds of problem areas. You must therefore prioritise: which three things would make the biggest difference to the student's performance? Language items? Behaviour? More homework? Participating more/less? and so on.

Prepare three key questions

You may have three things you want to say, but you should not have your conclusions prepared – after all, you haven't heard the student's point of view yet. So don't prepare your conclusions, but instead prepare three key questions that will make the student think about that area.

Not: *Your handwriting is terrible.*

But: *Did you know you may be losing marks because I can't read your answers?*

Not: *Stop speaking your own language when you're working in groups.*

But: *How can I band your speaking when you never use English naturally?*

Prepare your evidence

The student may not be aware he/she has the problem you want to discuss, or may deny he/she has the problem. You will therefore need concrete examples – pieces of work, or examples of specific events that happened in class – which you can use as 'evidence'.

TIP

If you don't want to keep massive files on each student, ask them to keep this evidence in their portfolios. Get the students to hand in their portfolio to you the previous lesson. On the other hand, the students may not keep 'bad' bits of work! You may need to keep these for them!

Prepare your lesson

In the lesson, you will need some uninterrupted time to do the interview. You will therefore need to prepare activities, e.g. getting groups to work on their projects, that the rest of the class can do without asking you for help or information. It is best to have group work: silent reading will mean all the students can hear your conversation and might make you and especially the student interviewee shy.

The interview: Suggested procedure

- Make sure that the rest of the class cannot hear the interview – it may make the student shy or embarrassed.
- Sit next to the student so that you can look at examples of work together.
- Produce a clean copy of the agenda, and quickly outline the stages.
- Use the students' L1 to make them feel comfortable – after all, we are talking about their performance, not doing an oral interview! On the other hand, if the students are capable of using English, all the better!

- Compare your agenda with the individual student's. If he/she has written nothing, he/she hasn't prepared the interview. Immediately stop the interview and re-schedule another date. There is no point negotiating plans if the student hasn't even thought about his/her responsibilities in the process. If this is a persistent problem, make it clear to the student that the review is itself part of his/her assessment.

- Ask how the (term) has gone.

  … Has it been similar to his/her plan or very different?
  … In what ways?
  … What is he/she happy with?
  … What is he/she unhappy with?
  … What problems is he/she having?

  Agree or disagree, either by asking (some of) your three questions, or by pointing out examples in his/her written work or classroom behaviour that confirm or contradict his/her views.

Note: The student may concentrate on things you had not predicted. If more important or useful issues arise, drop some or all of your three points.

- Ask what the student thinks you should both write as his/her goals (a maximum of three). Write them (if you agree – negotiate if you don't) on the plan in words that are as similar as possible to the ones he/she suggests. That way there can be no misunderstanding: it also gives you some idea of the students' way of describing problems and builds up your student-based vocabulary.

- Ask if there's anything else he/she would like to say, e.g. *Which bits of the lessons do you enjoy most/least? Do you like the coursebook? How do you get on with other people in the class?* etc. Treat him/her as a colleague discussing a work issue.

- Get the student to sign and date the sheet, thereby making a commitment.

- You should later photocopy this for his/her portfolio.

Possible problems and possible solutions

"What if the students can't understand the concept of appraisals?"

Roleplay or show a video of a typical APPRAISAL interview in front of the whole class before carrying out the first one. This will give them some idea of the structure of the interview.

Make sure the first interviewees are 'strong' personalities, because the rest of the class will ask them what happened, and you will need these first interviewees to give positive feedback to the rest of the class. If you can, video the interview to show a (different) class what interviews are like.

"What if the students cannot identify their strengths and weaknesses?"

This is almost certain to happen the first few times you have interviews. Remember that, for most students, the idea of being consulted is new to them. They are being asked to take on new responsibilities.

Here are some prompts you can use to help students during the interview. Ask:

- If they had a test tomorrow, what would they be most worried about?

- What would be easy?

- What do they do when they're working in groups:
  … give ideas?
  … do the writing?
  … put other people's ideas into correct English?

- Who is the best in their group or class? How do they know?
- If they are the best, what are they 'best' at? (This should give them an idea of different skills and abilities.)
- Tell them one area they are good at; ask for others.
- Ask them how they know if they've got better – apart from tests and homework marks. If they can't say, ask them which student they think has improved most over the (term). Ask them why.

"What if the students don't have enough language to express their ideas?"

They may have difficulty in expressing their ideas because this is not the kind of vocabulary area we often teach.

Do the interviews in the student's L1; or roleplay – live or on video/audio-tape – 'sample' APPRAISAL interviews. Treat these as listening comprehensions and present new/useful language. After all, APPRAISAL interviews are an excellent opportunity for real communication. Remember to include the language for planning as well as the language for reviewing.

Remember that there are three possibilities for the language used in the interview:

	Teacher	Student
a)	L1	L1
b)	L2	L1
c)	L2	L2

In addition, some parts of the interview can be in the L1 and other parts in the L2 (i.e. English).

"What if I don't have enough time?"

It is a well-known fact that SYLLABUSES expand to fill the time available! Many teachers will look at the example above and say *I haven't got enough time to teach the SYLLABUS, let alone dedicate all that time to reviews*. It is true that reviews do take up a lot of time. But it is important to remember the following.

- APPRAISAL interviews are an excellent opportunity for real teacher-student communication. How often now do your students have the chance to speak one-to-one with you? If the interview is done in English (by the teacher only, or by the teacher and the student), you are providing them with thousands of language-learning opportunities.
- Whichever language you use, there are also thousands of mutual learning opportunities – for both teacher and student. By encouraging them to think about and plan their learning, you are making the classes more efficient. From the interviews and the students' plans, you will be able to decide which items on the SYLLABUS can be dropped and which you need to concentrate on; and you will be able to assess your whole teaching programme and make it more efficient by matching the students' own language learning processes.
- There is an old saying: *Give a man a fish, and you feed him for a day; teach a man to fish, and you feed him for life*. APPRAISALS work in a similar way. It is always quicker and easier to do something yourself than teach someone else how to do it. But in the long term, it is better to make them independent. Who knows, in the long term, you may even save time. As we have seen in this book, students can begin to mark their own – or each other's – compositions; they even can write and mark each other's tests and exercises.

Summary

APPRAISALS and PERFORMANCE REVIEWS are becoming part of our working life. We have looked at why we do them, who does them, when they are done and what they consist of.

The following list details some of the information you could use when doing an appraisal for your students:

- results of 'formal' tests
- results of 'mini-tests'
- records of the student's homework – both results and frequency
- records of the student's attendance
- copies of the student's work displaying the student's strengths
- copies of the student's work displaying the student's weaknesses
- copies of any relevant BANDS and PROFILES
- copy of the course objectives, SYLLABUS, etc.
- notes concerning the student's contributions – good and bad – in class
- notes concerning the student's preferred learning style and strategies
- results of previous PERFORMANCE REVIEWS.

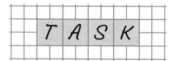

Can you set up an APPRAISAL system in your class? Can you start it this year or will you have to wait till next year? If you want to set one up, plan the following:

... how to organise the interviews
... what to ask students to bring
... what to bring yourself.

Good luck!

If you don't want to set one up, why not?

Time for a change?

In this book, we have looked at assessment: how we as teachers decide if a student is good or bad at English. We have seen that traditional tests can be very accurate and effective ways of measuring a student's abilities; but we have also seen a good test requires an enormous commitment in terms of time, personnel, expertise and money. Most schools do not have those resources, and so the kind of test we are able to write will never be sufficiently accurate to make important decisions about a student's future.

Think ...

Your job depends on your ability in English. Would you want a decision made about your employability based on your school's current test?

If it's not good enough for us, it may not be good enough for them ...

Also, we wouldn't want our ability assessed on the basis of two classroom observations. There are other important skills and other ways to measure them.

If it's not good enough for us, it may not be good enough for them ...

Each assessment procedure is, then, a problem that we have to solve. There is no ideal or perfect solution. Evaluation is about judgement: all we can do is to look at a wide range of evidence about a student's ability, listen to various interested parties, balance all the facts and opinions and make a decision. We must hope that that judgement is fair, and we may have to justify our decision at a later date. We must be accountable: to the school, to the parent, to the state and, most importantly, to the student.

If you have read this far, you may think that this all sounds a bit idealistic and impracticable. Let us look at these two problems separately.

"Is it idealistic?"   If the ideas in this book are idealistic, we are then saying the following.

- Our tests are best way we can think of to evaluate a student's performance.
- A student should only be assessed via formal tests.
- We can accurately turn a student's abilities into a set of numbers.
- The way a student learns is less important than the ability to remember facts.
- As teachers, we are more interested in testing knowledge than helping the student to learn.
- Only teachers can evaluate performance.
- The mark 13/20 is more useful to the student and their parents than a descriptive PROFILE or BAND.

"Is it impracticable?"   If the ideas in this book are impracticable, we are then saying the following.

- We would rather spend ten minutes marking the mistakes in a student's composition than talking to the student for ten minutes about his/her learning problems.
- The 30 minutes they spend writing this composition would give us a better idea of their abilities than the 15 minutes they spend writing their learner diaries.
- All students will intently study our corrections on their compositions and will learn a great deal from them.

- We will make a note of all the corrections we make on compositions so that we have a record of what the student's learning targets are.
- The multiple-choice test we write is a better tool for helping students to learn than the multiple-choice test they write for each other.
- A record of students' workbook exercise scores tells us more than what a student puts in their portfolio.

Do you agree?

The last chapter of this book ended: ... *students can begin to mark their own – or each other's – compositions; they even can write and mark each other's tests and exercises.* Some teachers will now say *But that's impossible!*

If you agree that this is impossible, write in each box why you feel this.

	compositions	tests	exercises
mark			
write			

Now look at your reasons. Can any of your reasons be overcome by teaching the students to do these tasks? How did you learn to do these tasks?

Teaching and evaluation

One last worry might be that all this evaluation is going to take up time that you should spend teaching.

"Is evaluation now more important than teaching?"

Well, in some ways, it is. Students are only able to learn by realising what they don't know and by recognising new items as being new. They need to experiment with new language to see where it is right or wrong. No teacher will ever be able to correct everything a student writes, says or, more importantly, understands. We already rely on the students being clever enough to **know** that they don't know – we rely on them saying *I'm sorry, but I don't understand.* This is how we learn: by asking questions.

Unfortunately, students rarely say *I don't understand.* They think that by admitting their lack of understanding, the teacher will think they are slow or stupid. So they just keep quiet and hope the teacher doesn't choose them to answer the question.

"Why is this?"

Because they fear getting the answer wrong, and they fear that the teacher will note this and give them a bad mark. They are not used to teachers asking them real questions. In other words, they don't say anything because they see the teacher's questions as tests.

In this way, testing may actually be preventing learning in our schools. Time for a change?

Syllabus item	What exactly are we teaching? (form, use, pronounciation?)	% of syllabus	Recognise (✓/X)	Produce (✓/X)	No. of items in test
Grammar:					
Vocabulary:					
Communication/ functions:					
Skills: reading writing listening speaking					
Other:					

2 Editing

Read this letter and mark each line right (✓) or wrong (✗). If there is a mistake, write the correct form or the missing word. Show where each missing word goes by writing a double slash (//). Show each wrong word by crossing it out.

Exercise

Line	Tick (✓) or cross (✗)	Correction
Dear Yukio		
Hello! My name is Rafael	✓	
and I am ✗ Spanish.	✗	
My teacher give me your name		
from a list of Japanese penfriends.		
I have 13 years old		
and I live in Zaragoza.		
Zaragoza is in the north of Spain		
and is a very beautiful city.		
There are four persons in my family.		
My father works on a bank		
and my mother is nurse.		
I have a sister, Alicia, who is six.		
We also have a dog called Pluto,		
but he is very old and a bit estupid.		
I like swimming and listening music		
and my favourite subject is history.		
Do you like music, too?		
What are your preferred groups?		
My teacher says that you live in Nagasaki.		
Is a nice place?		
Do you like to write to me?		
Please write soon.		
Best wishes		
Rafael		

ANSWER

Line	Tick (✓) or cross (✗)	Correction
Dear Yukio		
Hello! My name is Rafael	✓	
and I am ✗ Spanish.	✗	
My teacher give me your name	✗	gave
from a list of Japanese penfriends.	✓	
I have 13 years old	✗	am
and I live in Zaragoza.	✓	
Zaragoza is in the north of Spain	✓	
and is a very beautiful city.	✓	
There are four persons in my family.	✗	people
My father works on a bank	✗	in
and my mother is // nurse.	✗	a
I have a sister, Alicia, who is six.	✓	
We also have a dog called Pluto,	✓	
but he is very old and a bit estupid.	✗	stupid
I like swimming and listening // music	✗	to
and my favourite subject is history.	✓	
Do you like music, too?	✓	
What are your preferred groups?	✗	favourite
My teacher says that you live in Nagasaki.	✓	
Is // a nice place?	✗	it
Do you like to write to me?	✗	Would
Please write soon.	✓	
Best wishes		
Rafael		

CHANNEL 1

6.00	**News and Weather** Roundup of the latest world events
7.00	**Living Today** Channel 1's regular consumer advice programme
7.30	**EastEnders** London soap opera
8.00	**Football** First round of League Cup (details of teams to be announced)
10.00	**Comedy: They're All Crazy** Three crazy friends who share a flat. This week, Mary books a holiday.
10.30	**The Week in Politics**
11.00	**Film: Dirty Harry** Clint Eastwood as the hard-hitting detective
00.45	**Closedown**

CHANNEL 2

6.00	**Open University**
7.00	**Opera Now** Scenes from Rigoletto performed last week at La Scala
8.00	**Film: Terminator 2** He's back! Arnold Schwarzenegger returns in James Cameron's sequel to Terminator 1.
10.00	**Wildlife in Africa** Big cats: lions, leopards and cheetahs in their natural environment
11.00	**News and Weather**
11.30	**The Simpsons** An hour of fun with the American cartoon family
00.30	**Closedown**

MORE TV

6.00	**Walt Disney presents** An hour of your favourite cartoons
7.00	**International Darts**
8.00	**Soap Opera: The Loves of Lucinda** This week, Lucinda meets her Italian cousin, Marco.
8.30	**Miss Universe: live from Chile** The top beauty show to find the world's most beautiful woman
10.00	**News and Weather**
10.15	**Game Show Hour** *3-2-1* followed by *The Price is Right*
11.15	**Film: Ghostbusters** Comedy. New York is attacked by ghosts and only three men can save the city!
00.10	**Top of the Pops** The best of today's rock and pop music
00.45	**Closedown**

INDEPENDENT

6.00	**Wheels** The best in new cars and motor sport
7.00	**The World At War** Hitler invades Russia
8.00	**Films This Week** New releases reviewed by Pedro Sanchez
8.30	**The Book Programme** Televised interview with John Grisham
9.00	**News and Weather**
9.30	**Film: Gone with the Wind** The classic story of 19th century love and conflict in Georgia
00.30	**Closedown**

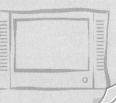

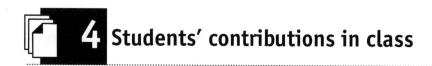
	Dates						
Name	1	2	3	4	5	6	7
	....	....	....	....	....	....	....
Accuracy in use of: structures pronunciation spelling							
Range of: structures vocabulary linkers socially appropriate language							
Ability to: interrupt and take turns listen to others							
Ability as a student: Do they contribute frequently? Do they use the target language when the teacher isn't listening?							
Other:							

LEARNER DIARY

Date: ....

Reading   coursebook/newspaper/magazine/reader/other: ....
Writing   exercises/composition/notes/letters/other: ....
Listening cassette/teacher/TV/radio/video/song/other: ....
Speaking groups/pairs/coursebook exercises/discussion/interviews/other:
....

Grammar:
   new
   revised	

Vocabulary:
   topic
   new words/phrases	

What we studied:	
What I learned:	
How I felt:	
Problems to ask about next time:	

Homework for next class: ....

Homework (last): ....   Marks/comments: ....

You may like to add other criteria on the lines provided.

Name:	Date							
	1	2	3	4	5	6	7	8
Accuracy: – structures – pronunciation – spelling – vocabulary								
Adequacy/Range: – structures – vocabulary – linkers/cohesion – social styles (friendly/polite) – ideas								
Contributions: – frequency – appropriacy – length								

APPRAISAL AGENDA

To: ....

Appraisal interview date: ....

I would like to talk about:

1 ....

2 ....

3 ....

You would like to talk about:

1 ....

2 ....

3 ....

Your last plan said you would look at:

1 ....

2 ....

3 ....

Ideas for your next plan:

1 ....

2 ....

3 ....

Your results so far this term

Checktests	Marks
....	....
....	....
....	....
Your homework average is	....

Attendance this year: .... classes out of ....

Please fill in the gaps and return this to me.

Remember to bring any work you want to show me, as well as your copy of the speaking and writing profiles in case we need to look at them.

Thank you.

Glossary

ACHIEVEMENT TESTS	These test whether students can do what they have been taught, either by testing specific SYLLABUS items or general objectives.
ANALYTIC MARKING SCHEMES	These try to break down marking into a number of different areas so that both teacher and student can see where they are successful and where the reader/listener has difficulties in understanding.
APPRAISALS	A system of reviewing a person's past, present and future – their work, their problems, their attitudes, etc.– leading from and to negotiated targets.
BACKWASH (OR WASHBACK)	The effect that a final test has on the teaching programme that leads to it – teaching to the test.
BANDING	This is similar to PROFILING, but normally describes the whole range of ability in the target language. Each BAND number refers to both DESCRIPTORS and relates to levels of ability. A BAND describes an ability level in any one skill, and therefore a writing band would include information concerning relevance, adequacy, grammar, etc.
CLINICS	Handing over a small part of the syllabus to the students. A section of a lesson (e.g. part of the last class part each month) is dedicated to questions that the students raise, like patients visiting the doctor.
CONFIDENCE RATINGS	These let you compare what the student can actually do with what he/she thinks he/she can do.
CONGRUENT EVALUATION	This looks at a whole process before it starts, in order to make sure that the aims, methodology and evaluation of the course match those stated.
CONSTRUCT VALIDITY	Does the test test the skills and items it's supposed to test and nothing else?
CONTENT VALIDITY	Does the test test the skills and items that it's supposed to test?
CONTINUOUS ASSESSMENT	This is no different from any other form of assessment – it simply refers to how frequently you test or evaluate the students. The student is assessed on not just one performance, but on many performances.
CRITERIA-REFERENCED TESTING	The result tells you about what the individual student can do, and does not compare him/her with other students. It describes certain criteria that the student has been able to meet.
CURRICULUM	The subjects that are studied in schools, and the procedures and approaches used to teach them. This is usually decided by the state.
DESCRIPTOR	One of several description levels of abilities for each sub-skill, e.g. *3 Complete understanding with appropriate vocabulary and few if any circumlocutions.*
DIAGNOSTIC TESTS	These use PROFICIENCY or ACHIEVEMENT TESTS to analyse strengths and weaknesses in the student or the teaching programme itself.
DIRECT TESTING	This means we ask the student actually to perform the skill we want to test. Compare INDIRECT TESTING.
DISCOURSE SKILLS	Making what we say fit what has been said before, or what is still to be said, e.g. I saw John. *He* said ..., not I saw John. *John* said ...
ENUMERATION	In general, the semi-scientific method used in testing of turning performances into numbers or results.
FACE VALIDITY	Does the test appear to test what it's trying to test?
FORMATIVE EVALUATION	This is the evaluation done and feedback gained during a process so that the process can be changed to make it more effective – to help this year's students rather than next year's.
HIGH/LOW CORRELATION	Is the test an extremely good indicator of the skill we are trying to test?

ILLUMINATION	Learning from doing something **with** the student, rather than doing something **to** the student, asking *How did you learn that? Why did you write that?*
INDIRECT TESTING	Testing things related to the skill we want to test in order to give us an indication of how the student would perform if they did the skill itself. Compare DIRECT TESTING.
NORM-REFERENCED TESTING	Using test results to compare the student with other students from that year and from other years. The result does not give any information about the student's individual performance, instead it compares him/her to the norm.
PERFORMANCE REVIEW	An interview with a superior leading to a document containing both a review of the past, as well as a plan for the future. This is a negotiated document – it is agreed and signed by both sides.
PLACEMENT TESTS	Used to put the student into a class or level depending on certain criteria.
PROFICIENCY TESTS	These test a general standard ability regardless of the teaching programme.
PROFILES	These break down marking into a number of different areas so that both teacher and student can see where they are successful and where the reader/listener has difficulties in understanding. Compare BANDS. PROFILES have several descriptions of abilities for each sub-skill. The technical term for each of these is a DESCRIPTOR.
QUALITATIVE DATA	Interest here is not so much in numerical results, but instead in the process.
QUANTITATIVE MEASUREMENT	In general, the semi-scientific method used in testing of turning performances into numbers or results.
RAW SCORES	Pure results given as numbers, before we convert them into a percentage, or a mark out of twenty, or an A-E grade.
RECOGNITION VS PRODUCTION	Some tests make students actively supply an answer (e.g. a gap-fill); while others simply ask students to recognise which answer is right (e.g. multiple-choice).
SALIENCY EFFECT	The experience, when learning a foreign language, of suddenly noticing an unknown word, phrase or construction being used time and time again. It suddenly becomes noticeable or 'salient' for a couple of weeks and then seems to disappear.
SCORER RELIABILITY	If you gave the same test to two different people to mark, would they give the same score? Is the marking objective or subjective?
STRATEGIC SKILLS	Such as how to take turns in speaking, get information from a text, listen for gist, etc.
SUMMATIVE EVALUATION	This is evaluation done and feedback gained at the end of (a stage of) a process. It looks at general feedback to the teaching procedure used, so that next year's course can be changed according to what has been more or less successful.
SYLLABUS	The outline of the course. This can be decided by the school management, government, individual teacher or by the coursebook.
TEST RELIABILITY	If it were possible to give the same person the same test (or a different version of it) at the same time, would the result be the same?
VALIDITY	See CONSTRUCT, CONTENT and FACE VALIDITY.

KEY TO TASK, PAGE 48

Here are three possibilities.

1 Tell the students to imagine they are in Britain and that their TV is broken: they can choose only one channel to watch all evening. In groups, they agree which channel they would choose, and say why.

2 Erase the names of some programmes, leaving only the descriptions. Ask the students to think of appropriate names for the programmes.

3 Ask the students to suggest which programmes specific people might watch, e.g. an elderly couple, a 12-year-old girl.

Further reading

House, S *An Introduction to Teaching English to Children* Richmond Publishing 1997
Chapter 14 looks at ways of evaluating children.

Hughes, A *Testing for Language Teachers* CUP 1989
A practical guide to issues in language testing, with exercises and suggestions for further reading, as well as useful appendices which explain statistics to beginners.

Simmons, H & Elliott, J (eds) *Rethinking Appraisal and Assessment* Open University Press 1989
This collection of articles by international contributors covers a wide range of issues, arguing that 'teacher appraisal and pupil assessment are inextricably linked.' Every page will get you thinking.

Index of topics

(numbers in brackets refer to photocopiable pages)